Transforming Teaching and Learning in Public Education

Dena R. Cushenberry
with
Leonard C. Burrello

ERP Books, Inc.

ISBN: 978-1-7324141-5-0

Printed in the United States of America
Book Designed by Jillian Goeler, Jag Ink

First Edition
10 9 8 7 6 5 4 3 2 1

Elephant Rock Books
Ashford, CT

For my sons, Adrian, Austin, and Charles; my
daughter-in-law, Chelsea;
my newest love, Aria Joy Cushenberry, and the entire
Armstrong and Burrello Families

TABLE OF CONTENTS

FOREWORD

In our twenty-four-hour news cycle, every topic is ephemeral, passed over for the next story that grabs the headline of the day or the hour. Education is a national treasure, too important for millions of children, parents, and communities to be left in the daily heap of "an old story." In this book, a former urban superintendent of a middle-to-large district of over twelve thousand students tells a story of transformational change in a minority-majority school system and the necessary orchestrations of leadership necessary to accomplish this change. Some key points are:

- The vision, sensitivity, caring, and communication from a great leader who made preparing all students to high levels an urgent collective endeavor.
- The Warren Way story details a long and deliberate intent that did not happen overnight. It prioritizes personalizing learning for both students and teachers. Its core value makes learning constant and time-variable an important concept for others to consider.
- A leader cannot do it alone. It takes the care and nur-

turing of a team of people to get it done.

- A set of issues that were confronted are common to-day—such as finding resources to support teacher re-cruitment and retention while reaffirming a culture of collaboration and teacher development.
- Getting a school board to suspend teacher evaluation based upon state accountability by emphasizing inter-nal accountability for student and teacher success by tracking district support to the classroom.

Many school district leaders fail to build a team of commu-nity leaders, businesspersons, school board members, school administrators, and teachers to embrace a vision for change. The "old way" stands in the way of change. Married to the old way are members from each constituency. This leader navi-gated those waters with vision, grace, and great skill. We all can learn from her on this, and her voice will carry well with current and aspiring superintendents.

The book opens with a very sad tale of the plight of public schools and the public's lack of trust in schools, school lead-ers, and teachers. It outlines very clearly the teacher shortage, the redirection of funding away from public schools, and the external pressures on schools and school districts to do more with less. The destabilizing impact of state policy that is creat-ing annual bouts of uncertainty and ambiguity is a substantial dimension of the argument that the authors outlines.

A story is embedded in each chapter that builds examples for others to emulate. The quotes from staff members add val-ue to the narrative. The "Lessons Learned" and "Reflection Questions" offer policy and practice recommendations that superintendents can use with district leadership teams and their Boards of Education. These lessons can also can work well in a class or training session for school leaders.

Two threads will be of concern to other superintendents: (1) On building capacity in people, including the board, administrative staff, teacher leadership, teachers, parents, and even students; (2) The "U-boat commanders" willing to sink the ship. As superintendent, Dena Cushenberry had to contend with and silence the latter. Talking about how she moved the vision and agenda forward with all the internal and external flack is a key part of a very good story told. Talking about the role of "keeper of the vision" is so important. When the crap hits the fan, Dena would be there to encourage and keep things rolling. How she removed people from the bus with grace is worth reading in itself.

The book closes with helpful items in the appendices. All in all this is a good read and a great story of success. It is always great to read good news!

Ronald Barnes
Director, BWP Associates
Professor Emeritus, Indiana University

CHAPTER ONE

The Superintendent Experience

Vertigo is defined as a "sensation of motion in which the individual or the individual's surroundings seem to whirl dizzily"; it is "a dizzy, confused state of mind." For educational leadership and governance in the public school system, this experience is born of the continuous disruption to local school district infrastructure, which affects policy, curriculum, instruction, assessment, personnel, funding, and organizational learning.

For over twenty years, my fellow superintendents and I have witnessed the steady erosion of public confidence in public schools. The constant churn of state policy standards and assessments lead both teachers and leaders to frequently reexamine curriculum, instruction, and evaluation of student learning and teacher competence. High-stakes teacher evaluations are designed, along with the draining of state resources, to finance the rise of charters, including funds for capital investments and other incentives to support private schools, which undermines the stability of public education. These two goals create instability in the teaching force and add to lowered student performance. In Michigan, for example, the state legislature limited the ability of local school districts to tax their residents to make up for funding shortfalls and deficits. In Indiana, the state legislature reduced the complexity index by more than 6 percent and gave those recovered dollars to the richer, higher-achieving suburban districts. Why this action? Who benefits from it?

The combination of state policy and funding challenges make leading a school district each year a major challenge for district leadership in the early twenty-first century. But the hardest impact fell on our teachers and school leaders who had to absorb the brunt of these challenges. Maintaining public support and trust in our schools is driven by the annual vertigo cycles.

This book was conceived to document the multiple transitions that educators endured while trying to educate a generation of students for uncertain futures. We have yet to understand the implications of these transitions on this generation of students. COVID-19 is but another challenge to find sufficient resources and the infrastructure to support appropriate technologies and ensure access for our teachers, parents, and children to learn remotely. The quality of remote learning is uneven and has caused a yearlong loss of student learning for many. We are still in the processing of learning the lasting impact of this lost year and its implications for teacher collaboration and development as well as the lack of social learning experiences for students with their peers. The lack of in-school support impacts food security, play, and physical exercise, all factors affecting a healthy lifestyle.

Our fear and consternation revolve around the loss of educator's voices in decision-making toward a constructive narrative of public schooling. Too often failure is defined solely by a zip code. This book offers an illustration of how one district transformed from a basic skills–scripted learning model to a personalizing learning module with rigor and critical thinking using emerging technologies to provide individualized anytime, anywhere learning for a new generation of digital learners. Our team created a learning community culture that was iterative and spiraling deeper, making learning constant and time variable for students, their teachers, and school leaders.

Finally, we wanted to celebrate the quality of our teachers and their success. We witnessed the constant recruitment of our teachers and school leaders by our more affluent neighbors who paid as much as $5,000 more for a teacher and up to $30,000 more for a school leader. We could not compete. But we could also welcome them back. We were always gratified when some of those teachers returned to our inclusive and learner-centered culture because they thought their teaching was more valued and more collaborative within their grade-level teams by school and across the district. Our district's focus and message was always, How can we get better and create the conditions for higher quality teaching and learning? Teacher recruitment and retention are huge issues in small and less affluent districts.

Writing this book gave us a chance to reflect upon a career and share the joy and privilege of leading a district team that came to believe in our moral purpose. Knowing the right thing to do required us to fulfill our purpose as educators to prepare students for futures that are unknown and unforgiving unless students can access a college education and/or careers that earn them a living wage. That preparation demands a curriculum and instruction that emphasizes skepticism in a world of alternative facts and opinions, critical thinking to manage the perspectives and the data that emerges, and the ability to reframe the problem or problematization to get to the under-lying threat to power, inequity, and inequality that divides our nation and the world communities into haves and have nots.

A Historical Picture

Schools have always been viewed as safeguards of societal safe-ty, stability, and civility. Since 1982, however, state and fed-eral policy makers have sought to disrupt the so-called "tide of mediocrity" that Secretary of Education Terrel Howard Bell once suggested was plaguing American public schools.[1] In practice, this has meant sowing the seeds of parent choice and privatization. This ideology, often called *neoliberalism*, is a political economic theory that posits that societal well-be-ing is best achieved by liberating individual entrepreneurial freedoms and skills within an institutional framework char-acterized by strong private property rights, free markets, and free trade. Anthropologist David Harvey adds that, because these freedoms are guaranteed in the marketplace under ne-oliberal policy, each individual is thus held responsible and accountable for his or her own actions and well-being.[2] These concepts of entrepreneurial freedom, strong private property rights, free markets, and personal accountability, he contends, extend into and affect all realms, including those of education, health care, and even retirement.[3]

Ultimately, however, the implementation of this ideology has led to disruption and a nearly perpetual wave of uncer-tainty and ambiguity, leading to chaos. We know that stable and consistent environments are needed to support student learning. Federal, state, and private-for-profit interests have become increasingly influential within the realm of public education. Reduced regulation of charter schools has fostered uneven competition between public education and other state-supported alternatives for students, money, and support—even when, oftentimes, those alternatives have not been held to the same expectations and accountability to adequately and equally service all students and their families. In sum, public accountability is, only naturally, often absent in an era of privatization. Yet public accountability levied by state and federal mandates has increased since 2002 over public schools.

The truth, however, of how district leaders must respond in these turbulent and disruptive times can be found in the same place as always: in the creation of conditions for student success at the local school and classroom levels. We believe school districts across the nation have had to develop responses to state and federal mandates that have impacted local funding of education, teacher preparation, promotion, salary, and retention of quality teachers, student and teacher assessments, and other accountability measures that are not related to preparing students for post-school life in the twenty-first century.

The Guises of School "Choice"

We often hear about the amount of resources it takes to educate children in urban schools in disadvantaged areas, especially those characterized as "failing." Public schools are being structurally dismantled by the political "gift" of school choice and bias access to for-profit companies disguised as turnaround school improvement options for "failing schools." In reality, this is an assault on public education—the institution that never has turned its back on children in any of its communities.

This assault erodes the commitment to build a public and civic society that is increasingly diverse and inclusive. Over the last five years, we have seen the impact of divisive national leadership eroding community institutions and structures and well-being. From health care to policing to education, a true public requires common experience and association, allowing relationships between different social classes and races and the ability to live together in common spaces.

The American cultural critic Neil Postman wrote that schooling is about making a life, not just making a living. He argued it is "the central institution through which the young might find reasons for continuing to educate themselves."[4] This purpose for schooling, along with the need to create an equitable society whose members respect and care for one another, are two of the most significant antidotes to what we are witnessing in our divided and polarized nation today.

We know private school choice vouchers, charter schools, and other for-profit entities have been touted as better educational options for students in urban areas where there are a large number of "D" and "F" schools (covered in greater depth in chapter 2). Most of the for-profit options are companies that enter these vulnerable communities with little or no understanding of their traditions and customs. They have little knowledge of the culture and norms as they attempt to "turn around" these schools. The general public has been led to believe that public education in their communities is failing their children through political zip code reports. Intentional state policy that pushes school choice through charters and for-profit vendors as a better option for students only devalues public schooling.

USA Today reported in 2013 that the Indiana state supreme court ruled unanimously that tax dollars may be used to finance private school tuition under the state's voucher program. The ruling on a teacher's union–supported lawsuit from 2011 ends the legal challenge to the broad program at the state level. Indiana cites, "We hold that the Indiana school voucher program, the choice scholarship program, is within the legislature's power under Article 8, Section1." The case began after the program was created in 2011 when a group of teachers, school officials, and parents who opposed vouchers sued the state, arguing the program was unconstitutional. Vouchers allow low-income families to redirect tax dollars from their local public school district to pay tuition when children transfer to private schools. These actions have been allowed in states around the country.

All parents want their child's future to be brighter and more fulfilling than their own. So, when they are promised a better educational opportunity, they are likely to consider that option seriously. But how does this choice impact the neighborhood schools? Namely, it impacts funding, community relationships, teacher recruitment, and so on. Those charters take enrollment from the public schools and the tuition money attached to those students moving to charters or private schools. Private school vouchers dismantle and destabilize the support structure of the local public school district. Clearly, many public schools can do better, but when resources are taken from our most vulnerable schools and given to charters, private, for-profits, and wealthier districts, how can those vulnerable schools have an equal chance for success? From the School Choice Fact Sheet in 2019, we learn that there are fifty-six publicly funded private school choice options in twenty-six states, DC, and Puerto Rico. These schools are serving over five hundred thousand students and have doubled since 2012. There are eight types of programs that filter public money to these choice programs. The table below offers a snapshot of typical choice programs.

Types of Publicly Funded Choice Programs	
Educational Savings Accounts: Parents choose approved educational expenses placed in an account to customize a program for their child in six states	Scholarship Tax Credit Programs: States provide incentives for business and individuals to donate to non-profit organizations to provide scholarships to students in eighteen states.
Voucher Programs: Dollars follow the child, allowing parents to choose a private school and receive a state-funded scholarship to pay tuition in thirteen states and Washington, DC.	Parental Tax Credit Programs: Individual state income tax credits that include private school tuition in two states only.

Charter Schools: Public schools run by educators and community bodies, which promote innovative and specialized educational programs.	Public School Choice: Open enrollment that allows students attending poorly performing schools to attend higher performing schools inside or outside their assigned school district.
Course Choice: Allows K-12 public and private providers to enroll in individual course options using state funds offered in traditional and online blended formats.	Virtual Schools: Allows students to take one or all school courses online.

We know it is hard to educate a child living in poverty. There are more health, economic, transportation, and household needs; deeper needs for a safe and nurturing upbringing; and certainly often, more hunger. But, with high quality, well-paid teachers and a safe school environment that attends to nutrition and health needs, these students can learn and thrive. They may not learn at the same rate, time, and/or the same way, but all students can learn, especially with personalized teaching and the support to become self-directed learners through targeted instruction incorporating digital content tailored to their developmental level.

So, this is about—politics!—the elimination and reduction of public resources and pay for teachers who make a difference in the daily lives of students. The current climate is to privatize as much of the public education sector as possible to dilute its political influence in the local community. The struggle for control over the public's purse strings leads to maintaining inequity through reducing financial resources for low-socioeconomic districts without political leaders with influence who can fight for those communities.

The voucher money pouring into private schools in the name of helping underprivileged students is criminal. Steve Hinnefeld, in his blog, *School Matters: K–12 Education in Indiana*,[5] states that Indiana Republican legislators are proposing to increase state funding for some students who receive state-funded vouchers to attend private schools. "They want to add a new category of voucher, bridging the gap between low-income families that qualify for 'full vouchers' and middle-income families that get 'half vouchers.' Currently, students who qualify by family income for free or reduced-price school lunches qualify for a voucher worth 90 percent of state per-pupil funding received by their local public school district. A family of four could make up to $58,000 a year and qualify for the 70-percent voucher. At current funding levels," he continues, "that voucher would be worth about $3,700 per child, on average. I'm guessing it would pay close to the full cost of tuition at many private religious schools in Indiana," allowing parents to move their student to a private school. The public school in the area of the private school is responsible for providing service to private school special education and the students the school deems having difficulty learning. These are additional Title I and special education funds that are being siphoned from programs at the district level.

To add insult to injury, this spring of 2021, in House Bill 1005, the Indiana legislature is proposing $202 million for private school voucher expansion, the total remaining of $175 million is to be distributed to the 291 school districts that serve 96 percent of the student population. This allows families with a combined income of $145,000, which is twice the state's median family income, to participate in the program.

The Warren team believed the answer to the change in complexity index was to find education advocates in the community willing to run for local and state office to challenge state representatives and legislators who limit public school support. As superintendents, we know that after a charter school is closed in a district and resources have been allocated for the year, they return to the local district (after the state has allocated money for districts for the year based on a September enrollment count ADM) without the dollars following that student for that year. This happens over and over in Indiana and across the nation. Every student in America deserves a great school regardless of location. Every school deserves to have a good teacher in every classroom who is paid a living wage.

The Warren Township Response

Across the country, the economy is changing. Innovation and STEM programs are at the forefront of conversations about the unemployable workforce in America. New technologies have yielded few opportunities for bygone industrial communities left behind, ravishing the spirit of lower- and middle-class families. Few communities have the infrastructure to coordinate with businesses and offer a career education to accommodate this ever-changing shift in demand. Warren is a school district that in the nineties had a 98 percent graduation rate with 20 percent of families living in poverty. Today's graduation rate is 89.7 percent with the help of student access to evening and night school for credits recovery. The poverty level surpasses 75 percent. The number of students qualifying for free and reduced-price lunches is 78 percent, meaning the district is considered high poverty.[6]

I was a superintendent for six years, assistant and deputy superintendent for four. I came from a middle school assistant principalship and opened an elementary school and within five years the school community celebrated the honor of being a National Blue Ribbon School. The district team uncovered issues that our district was wrestling with over the past ten years. The team navigated these turbulent times by creating innovative local responses to advance our goals for preparing students for post-school life. I have identified the lessons learned as we confronted eight challenges and offer the implications for others to consider in moving their districts forward toward their own ascending innovative learning models and goals for district, school, teacher, and student success.

I have included my Warren Township district team's research, which was used to inform the work of others, templates for district narratives, and frameworks for planning and organizing district work from the central office to the classroom for others to emulate. This book captures how a collaborative district leadership team came together to build a coherent message that connected students, staff, and community in a common pursuit of transformative purpose for learning. Specifically, I suggest that this book's distinctive contributions include how to respond to a sample of needs and issues common to many districts.

If schools are indeed to be the safeguards of safety, stability, and civility, as superintendents, we must prioritize the well-being of students through positive dispositions toward learning and leading a fulfilling life; through prioritizing high levels of student engagement with learning, with their schools, and with their communities; with caring student and adult relationships forming the foundation of in-school life; through purpose-driven, meaningful learning and a commitment to post-graduate success; and, finally, by establishing accomplishment in academic, social, and extracurricular arenas as the chief goal for every student.

These eight challenges serve as the foundation of the book; each chapter is devoted to one challenge. The issues my district dealt with demonstrate how, as a superintendent with district-level colleagues and school principals, we thrived in a highly collaborative culture driven by a clear purpose, bounded by a set of core values, and guided by a powerful mission to prepare students for success in college and beyond. With this book, I sought to capture a leadership-based educational phenomenon, which is often found but less often documented. In this district case study, I hope you find inspiring leadership practices initiated by leaders in our cabinet, principals, and instructional specialists, who came together and created a personalized learning environment for teachers and students alike. This was an environment infused with technology, clever opportunism, and a positive, cooperative, and appreciative use of all the district's human resources and capital. It was an environment driven by and built around a philosophy of continuous improvement of teaching and learning practices.

I believe this book demonstrates that local leadership matters at every level of a school system, and that the best leadership is driven by a positive and optimistic vision of the future and a concrete set of internal core values to guide decision-making processes from the level of the school board and district office to the levels of individual schools and classrooms. Stability of leadership, combined with a data-driven teaching staff, helped this district to accomplish the goals it set for itself. Internal accountability in the public sector is what matters most—not the pressures of external forces. For if we are to function in a neoliberal era of loosened marketplace constraints and expanded personal accountability, then we need to conceptualize a school district as an individual, one whose duty is to be personally accountable to itself when the federal government won't hold it to the necessary standards.

I wrote this book with the support of my colleague and husband, Leonard Burrello, an emeritus professor at Indiana University and still a courtesy professor at the University of South Florida. He analyzed the data with an external researcher, which led to the district team's themes that are the foundation of this book. I cannot thank him enough for helping me share this district case study over the entire ten-year period this book covers. This book is dedicated to the Warren District team and those who follow.

Let's begin.

References

1   *A Nation at Risk: The Imperative for Educational Reform: A Report to the Nation and the Secretary of Education, United States Department of Education*, prepared by the National Commission on Excellence in Education (Washington, DC: 1983).

2   David Harvey. *A Brief History of Neoliberalism.* New York: Oxford University Press, 2005.

3   American Federation for Children. "The School Choice Fact Sheet 2019."https://www.federationforchildren.org/wp-content/uploads/2016/09/AFC-School-Choice-Fact-Sheet-6-2019.pdf.

4   Neil Postman. *The End of Education: Redefining the Value of School.* New York: Knopf, 1995.

5   Steve Hinnefeld. "School Voucher Surprise," *School Matters: K–12 Education in Indiana* (blog), February 19, 2019, https://inschoolmatters.wordpress.com/2019/02/19/school-voucher-surprise/.

6   Dena R. Cushenberry, Warren Township, Superintendent Report to the Board of Education, 2017–18.

CHAPTER TWO

Changing State Standards and Assessments

It's a challenge, contending with federal and state laws that often work against the public education system. We're always trying to shield our staff from them—from impersonal statewide accountability measures to statewide assessment measures that don't take into account the unique contexts of each district. —Brian Simkins, Human Resource Director

The vertigo and what caused it: The constant churn of state policy with regard to academic standards and assessments that cause both teachers and school leaders to reexamine curriculum, instruction, and evaluation of student learning and teacher competence.

Almost all challenges outlined in this text can be traced back to state policy changes related to accountability, teacher evaluation, student assessment, and funding. Each of these

factors influenced how the district leadership team responded to them as part of our continuous improvement process.
The impact each new policy change had on subsequent district implementation and ongoing operations is the focus of
this book. These state changes were inspired by federal policy
that affected all school districts and required internal district
responses from all types of school district—rich, poor, high, or
lower achieving. Warren is but one example of how one highly
stable district handled the impact of state policy and funding
on its vision, purpose, and core values over a ten-year period.

A stable district is one with a continuity of leadership that
embraces a set of common values and pursues a set of goals
over time using empowering processes that create conditions
for quality teaching and learning. Stable districts have significant and supportive relationships with their students, parents,
teachers, and principals. Their leadership is known inside and
outside the system and is seen as a coherent group of decision-makers connected to their community.

My successor and current superintendent in Warren Township noted that the state had changed its assessment plans three
times in the past five years, and I added two more times in a
previous five-year period. Finances and funding of local schools
changed at least twice during the ten-year time frame, all requiring the district to respond by tightening its fiscal belt. Multiple sets of state standards and assessments form the context
of vertigo. It required district leadership dialogue and action
to maintain equilibrium and to thrive in a turbulent economic
and state policy environment. This began with the 2008–2009
national recession that impacted school funding in 2010 and
has reemerged during this Covid-19 pandemic period.

The pandemic increased the inequity of Internet access,
which impacts remote education and student learning, along

with economic insecurity and family destabilization. In an August 2020 United Nations report it was noted that "The COVID-19 pandemic has created the largest disruption of educational systems in history, affecting nearly 1.6 billion learners in more than 190 countries and all continents. Closures of schools and other learning spaces have impacted 94 per cent of the world's student population, up to 99 per cent in low and lower-middle income countries."[1] Local boards of education must be an integral part of the dialogue to ensure community support as districts respond during the pandemic.

Indiana and the Common Core State Standards (CCSS)

Starting in 2010, forty-five states adopted the CCSS benchmark, which spelled out what students from kindergarten through high school should learn and be able to do in reading and math. With minimal objection, Indiana joined twenty-five states, including New York, Tennessee, and Colorado, in affiliating with the Partnership for a National Assessment of Readiness for College and Careers (PARCC) system. Michigan, California, and twenty-eight other states went with the Smarter Balanced Assessment Consortium based in Minnesota.

As the political winds shifted, the Common Core backlash ensued with vigor, much of the opposition fueled by Tea Party–aligned groups. By 2014, the CCSS standards were under fierce political attack, facing repeal in many states. As Common Core became politically toxic, state legislatures across the country voted to pull out of the Common Core and PARCC testing consortia, Indiana being the first, but they all eventually kept 80 to 90 percent of the original standards. For example, Florida kept all the standards but added cursive writing and something like fifty calculus standards.

Elitist Intervention

In conjunction with the Common Core movement and state standards and assessment, a focus on the charter school movement became the driving force for school privatization. The narrative of public education became "schools are failing our most vulnerable students and parents should be given choice to go and find a private or public school charter to serve them."

Politicians used this as an opportunity to define public schools as government schools, which deepened a lack of trust in the ability of the schools to serve all students well. By offering privatization as a solution that solves the crisis of underfunding and teachers exiting the profession, legislatures used the charter school movement to reduce the overall funding of public education. The key driving forces for austerity and the privatization agendas are similar across all states that have seen strikes (Arizona, Colorado, Kentucky, Oklahoma, and West Virginia). No state dropped as much academically as Michigan. Under No Child Left Behind, states began to argue for more accountability through standards-based learning and assessment to grade schools and to close failing schools while opening up choices (competition) and more funding and support for private and parochial schools. This phenomenon started in Minnesota, then spread to Arizona, Florida, and Michigan. No place has been more scrutinized as to this move's effects on student learning and support for public education than Michigan. See Mark Binelli's report in the *New York Times*,[2] Shawn D. Lewis's article in the *Detroit News*,[3] and the Education Trust's report on what it characterizes as a broken promise.[4]

Molly Gott and Derek Seidman point out the three groups that are the main problem for public education: billionaire school privatizers, regional corporate forces, and Koch-backed think tanks.[5]

In a 2015 *Fortune* article entitled "How Business Got Schooled in the War Over Common Core,"[6] Peter Elkind states, "When Exxon Mobil, GE, Intel and others pushed for the new state education standards, they incurred the wrath of the Tea Party conservatives and got a painful lesson in modern politics." Other powerful interest groups wanted less investment, both to lower state taxes for public education and to ensure education receives a smaller portion of public resources. Decreasing funds for public schools would preserve the inequality that already exists between urban and rural America—wealthier suburbs get to stay within their tax base to maintain high-quality education opportunity and access to post-secondary education. Certain players wanted to maintain the segregation of the rich and the poor and keep working-class people poorly educated to do the jobs needed to run their industrial and commercial enterprises.

In addition, these researchers posit that the teachers' strikes in West Virginia, Arizona, and Oklahoma in 2019 represented a major pushback by public workers against the right-wing agenda of austerity and privatization. They believe that privatization agendas influenced the 2017 corporate tax cuts for corporations, who then use declining tax revenue as a rationale to cut funding for state-funded services like public schools.

A nice summary of these corporate titans' emergence has been documented by Kurt Andersen in *Evil Geniuses: The Unmaking of America in* 2020,[7] which ties the Koch brothers (oil barons) and other ultraconservatives' lack of active participation in the national political discourse to a 1971 memo prepared by former Supreme Court justice Lewis Powell. Powell chastised corporate leaders for failing to foresee a revolution against the free enterprise system by the liberal left. He proposed that "they weaponize their philanthropic giving in order to fight a multifront war of influence over American political thought." Powell went on to propose "waging this war on four fronts—in academia, the media, politics, and the legal system—and doing so with unheard of budgets and ferocity." He notes that the "judiciary may be the most important instrument for social, economic and political change" (58). Powell calls this "a vast area of opportunity, if businesses is willing to provide the funds" (59). Hence Citizens United emerged as a major weapon to impact the political process and the pursuit of their agenda.

This is the beginning of the destruction of many American institutions preceding the Reagan administration and the tide of mediocrity narrative and the start of educational vertigo. Andersen writes that Reagan studied at the feet of Powell and Milton Friedman before becoming president.

The Fight for Higher Standards and Depth of Knowledge

As a superintendent, I believed, along with two of the state's major university representatives and the Urban League, the PTA, and other teachers' and administrators' associations, that we should stay with the Common Core because of the rigor we all saw in the CCSS. I also argued that any set of new standards must reflect CCSS since they were aligned with the SAT and ACT—extremely important for our high school students in Indiana. If we failed to align any new standards with those college exams, Indiana students might be penalized for low performance due to alignment issues, which might impact student scholarships.

My argument was that the Common Core, PARCC, and Smarter Balanced would make everyone accountable for educating *all* students in America at a high level. CCSS was superior in preparing the next generation's standards for college and career readiness. Early in the transition process we noticed that the depth of knowledge built in the CCSS standards was rigorous.

Lesson learned—we lost the fight. Like those local districts in New York and Illinois before us.

Seeing the landscape that was emerging, we decided the best way for our district to build on our current investment in the CCS work was to offer our teachers to the state's "Hoosier for Hoosier" standards committees. This would allow for an inside look into the upcoming (financial) changes. They found that 90 percent plus of the Common Core standards remained in the Indiana standards adoption—this clearly was not a fight about education standards. Most concerning, the state legislators did not see spending money for contracting a new vendor test to be of concern. Twenty-three million dollars spent to create a new assessment would have been better spent increasing the pay of teachers. The initial cost of PARCC and Smarter Balanced to states would had been zero. Vendor-driven decision-making versus what school leaders think is best for their students under those new standards drove decision-making.

Warren's Transformation

My predecessor as superintendent laid out the governor's plan and sought an instructional strategy in 2003 based upon management consultant William Edwards Deming's work on total quality management business model that emphasizes (Plan, Do, Check, Act) and imported the eight-step process from Texas (more below). At the time, I had just been appointed as a new school principal. This process became the ascending loop of innovation and discarding the descending loop of tracking and pigeonholing students to their assumed ability levels. The district, with its high poverty rate, brought the eight-step process to scale and competed statewide with our nine peer districts in Marion County, Indiana, largely because of the district's and principal's commitment and the infrastructure that was built to support teacher development and *implementation* through a district instructional support team of outstanding teachers.

In 2012-13 when I became superintendent the district team started a discussion of the need for a deeper and more critical evidence-based response to teaching and learning. The initial transformation from Loop One (the descending instructional practice), known as the eight-step process, and its focus on basic skills (tests and letter grades), to Loop Two (the ascending, innovative practice), which is personalized learning (college and career readiness), and our focus on the Core 4—targeted/small group instruction, integrated digital content, data-driven/data-informed observation, and student reflection and ownership—was preceded by the state's and district's preoccupation with responding to new Common Core standards. Thus, our district team started to repurpose the district core model of instruction and establish its core values in pursuit of that purpose and our vision statement for 2025. The new ascending change loop was now personalizing learning and the infusion of integrated technology. The descending loop was now standardized-based instruction and assessment. The best way to visualize and to understand the change is through a Theory of Change illustrated by the Two Loops Model from the Berkana Institute founded by Margaret J. Wheatley and Deborah Frieze.

In this model, the descending loop represents a state-based accountability system driving the quality of curriculum, formative assessment, and instruction downward by reducing students to fungible, interchangeable storehouses of information to be taught in the same way and according to the same time schedule and a rigid set of external standards and assessment mechanisms.

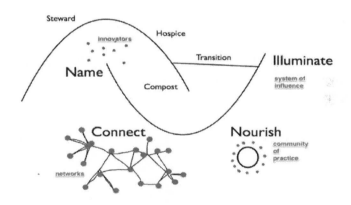

Meanwhile, the ascending loop represents a student-centered, transformative learning system that changes and improves curriculum, assessment, and instruction on a daily basis by emphasizing personalized learning. It starts with the mindset that instruction is paced to individualized learning preferences and interests that appeal to each student in terms of their own learning plan. The premise then becomes that learning is constant, and the time necessary for any individual to learn a specific body of knowledge or skill or method is variable. Teaching each student how he or she learns is paramount so that every student can become the architects of his or her own learning. In addition to providing the contrast between ascending and descending platforms, the figure displays how various actor roles interact in the transition from one platform to another. This change process is complex and demands that leaders respect where different staff and stakeholders reside in that transition from one loop to the next.

Prior to my staff's work to implement the Common Core standards effectively into Warren's schools, the district was following the trajectory of the descending loop. It was driven by state standards and using formative assessment processes derived from those standards. Instructional practices were tied to a three-week process that placed students in one of three categories: "enriched" (meaning the students who successfully mastered the three-week assessments); "in need of more practice" (those students who partially mastered the three-week assessments); or "remedial" (students who failed to pass the three-week assessments).

In order to extract ourselves from this loop, my cabinet and selected teaching staff researched the Common Core State Standards. Along with innovators in the state Department of Education, we created a growing group of forward-thinking educators who developed crosswalks of PARCC and Smarter Balanced Assessment Consortium, searching for a testing system that could match the new Common Core State Standards as they developed. A new, ascending loop emerged, one that offered new possibilities and the opportunity to personalize student learning according to more rigorous standards.

The ascending loop of personalized learning was the means to give teachers a voice in their own development and to retain quality teachers in a time of fiscal retrenchment. The board's endorsement of a resolution to pursue internal values as the metrics of success for students, teachers, and principals represented their support for this future. As federal and capitalist forces gave way to ripple effects at the local level, Warren rolled with the punches. David Holt, assistant superintendent for business and finance in Warren, summed it up best: "Every year, you come to know more and more about changing federal and state mandates and those outside of what we do every day who are telling us how to do our jobs—those are the greatest challenges."

To hold ourselves accountable, the district team shared with the Board of Education an alternative set of measures to assess our student performance. We developed over the 2014–15 school year a local report card that used the following assessments to measure the degree to which individual schools and the district were accomplishing the five items listed below:

Report Card Focus Area	Assessments
Personalized learning	The level at which "Student Will" behaviors are enacted to increase student voice and choice

Graduation rate	Graduation rate (target improvement 88–90 percent)
Reducing the Achievement Gap	Measuring academic achievement gap by student subgroup. Student Literacy Performance on the Indiana IREAD-3 assessment
Student Literacy	Performance on Indiana IREAD-3 assessment
College and Career Readiness	College and career dual credit and certifications rate above 25 percent; State criteria yet to be determined

With destabilizing factors out of their control, leadership must find a way to make sense of the sometime unexplainable motives and actors at the state level. The above criteria was our way of staying focused on the important work of our district's school system, which was to educate every student every day like they were our own.

Using this criterion, we moved all schools forward in personalized learning. We created the condition for student and teacher choice, and through reflection and ownership, students now have a better understanding of how they can grow. The graduation rate in 2012–13 was 84.3 percent, and in 2015–16, increased to 90.2 percent. Third grade reading scores at our lowest performing school, Sunny Heights, increased over two consecutive years, from 81.6 in 2013–14 percent and to 86 percent in 2014–15 (Indiana Department of Education Compass). However, it's important to note that even as we tried to account for changing state standards by making our own criteria, state and federal forces trumped all. In 2018, the high school graduation rate dropped from 90 percent to 80 when the state changed the criteria for what constituted a high school graduate. We did our best to prepare for these fluctuations that were out of our control.

Looking Back and Forward

In a stable district, culture grows slowly and evolves even slower. Programming and personnel changes might affect the climate, but culture changes only over time. Culture is deeply embedded in the norms and values expressed in decisions and overt actions of its organizational members. The bond between the board and its leadership and staff constitutes the district culture. This bond is essentially a moral contract in pursuit of communal, not individual, purposes. Having a moral lens ensures community norms around loyalty, cooperation, forbearance, honesty, equality, fairness, and compassion; it supports their implementation, as well as the newer values of civility, trust, respect, collaboration, resilience, hope, and community. Vibrant culture actors look out for challenges to their vision and mission.

Constancy of Purpose

Let me close out our transformative work with research on the significance of a district vision and commitment along with the necessary educational infrastructure to bring a change to scale. James Spillane, Megan Hopkins, and Tracy Sweet[9] offer practical implications of their research to school districts that mirror the practices that we implemented. They offer this advice to transform instruction in your school district.

First, settling on a vision for instruction is foundational for any effort to redesign educational infrastructure for supporting instruction and its improvement. Second, though standards or curriculum and student assessments have dominated conversations about improving instruction, especially at the state and federal levels, our analysis shows that building an educational infrastructure to support instruction and instructional improvement involves much more, including formal positions (like instructional specialists) and organization routines (like coaching or PLCs). Third, thinking systematically about how various components of an educational infrastructure work together (or not) to influence teachers' interactions about instruction and its improvement and the focus and depth of these interaction is essential. Focusing on one or two components (e.g., curriculum, coaching) in isolation fails to take advantage of how components of the educational infrastructure work interactively to structure teacher and peer interactions about instruction.

Lessons Learned

Internal versus External Accountability
- The local board and the superintendent need to be on the same page regarding how they measure district success.
- The district is always responding to three sets of accountability systems that may not be aligned, from the local board representing the community at large to the state department of education to the federal department of education.
- Think about how you determine the meaning of success—what does smart and talented mean? Does it include the ability to sort fact from fiction? And how does your definition of success demonstrate or predict the likelihood of producing a society of well-educated, law-abiding, and productive citizens?

Managing Change Loops
- Managing descending and ascending change requires recognizing "why" we are changing; what is being added, modified, or replaced; existing practices and "how" might we proceed with minimal disruption to the system. Who best leads the effort at every level of the system and how is it communicated to all stakeholders? How will the innovation answer the essential question: Will it improve teaching and learning?
- Always search for and build innovation with the positive core of your staff who have demonstrated strength and resilience to lead a change effort. Agree upon a theory action that views implementation as a learning process.

Coherence and Connectedness
- A district needs an inspiring core purpose and set of in-

ternal values supporting its vision of the future to motivate and sustain teacher and student learning. Teachers stay connected to transformative change only when they are trusted, respected, and supported by district action.

Leadership
- Listening to all stakeholders and asking what we are missing or what we are not seeing that impacts district and school success. Always ask who is not benefiting and why?
- A commitment for everyone's success in the organization
- Success is bigger than any one person; expect the expertise to emerge in all places, and distribute leadership throughout
- Building on teacher and staff strengths and collaboration with others is the secret to our success in this transformation.

District and Community
- Knowing and respecting the history of the community while trying to explore the future together.
- The district must demonstrate its commitment to community well-being through its academic and non-academic programs.
- Learn how the community supports students during after-school hours.

Reflection Questions

1. What historical challenges has your district team faced? To what extent did those challenges and your response cause you to defer or initiate action, reduce or add programming, and lose or attract quality staff? Can you identify some of the consequences of those actions, either positive or negative?
2. How might an inventory of challenges and decisions help you understand what a district has accomplished that is positive and illustrates its strengths and potential? What are the root causes of the district's success?
3. How might this chapter inform you and your school district team as you reflect on the challenges and choices before you today? What are the sources of those challenges? Internal or external? Can you cite and describe the antecedent conditions? What did you anticipate or what did you miss?
4. Most importantly, can you identify the positive core of staff who have the expertise to help move the district into the future? How prepared are you to distribute leadership responsibility and authority to those who can initiate and lead the change desired?
5. Once this review is well on its way, can you start to simultaneously discover your long-term purpose and core values in order to establish a focus on the future?
6. Upon review of your own responses to challenging issues or events, have you clearly identified the role you played as a district leader and other leaders at the school and classroom levels?

7. Finally, might you consider the Berkana's Institute's principles that underly all that they do, in your transformative work in the future?

a. Whatever the problem, community is the answer.

References

[1] United Nations. "Policy Brief: Education during COVID-19 and Beyond," August 2020, https://www.un.org/development/desa/dspd/wp-content/uploads/sites/22/2020/08/sg_policy_brief_covid-19_and_education_august_2020.pdf.

[2] Mark Binelli. "Michigan Gambled on Charter Schools. Its Children Lost," *New York Times Magazine*, September 5 2017, https://www.nytimes.com/2017/09/05/magazine/michigan-gambled-on-charter-schools-its-children-lost.html.

[3] Shawn D. Lewis. "Michigan Test Score Gains Worst in Nation," *Detroit News*, February 20, 2017, https://www.detroitnews.com/story/news/local/michigan/2017/02/20/michigan-test-score-gains-worst-nation/98144368/.

[4] The Education Trust–Midwest. "Accountability for All: The Broken Promise of Michigan's Charter Sector," February 2016, https://midwest.edtrust.org/wp-content/uploads/2013/10/The-Education-Trust-Midwest_Accountability-for-All-2016_February-11-2016.pdf.

[5] Molly Gott and Derek Seidman. "A Guide to the Corporations that Are De-Funding Public Education & Opposing Striking Teachers." LittleSis, May 14, 2018, https://news.littlesis.org/2018/05/14/a-guide-to-the-corporations-that-are-de-funding-public-education-opposing-striking-teachers/.

[6] Peter Elkind. "How Business Got Schooled in the War Over Common Core," *Fortune*, December 23, 2015, https://fortune.com/longform/common-core-standards/.

[7] Kurt Andersen. *Evil Geniuses: The Unmaking of America–A Recent History*. New York: Random House, 2020.

8   Berkana Institute, The Two Loop Theory. Berkana.org.

9   James P. Spillane, Megan Hopkins, and Tracy M. Sweet. "School District Educational Infrastructure and Change at Scale: Teacher Peer Interactions and Their Beliefs About Mathematics Instruction," *American Educational Research Journal* 55, no. 3 (June 2018): 532–62.

CHAPTER THREE

Redistricting: A Response to Funding Challenges

In the 2009–10 school year, Dena led the charge of closing two schools while we were going through a major population shift of students in the community and in a state context that was complex and constantly changing. It was a negative atmosphere for public education and for our community.—Tim Hanson, Superintendent

The vertigo and what caused it: What is the state education policy agenda behind the draining of state resources? Financing the rise of charters, including funds for capital investments and other incentives to support private schools, which undermines the stability of public education.

The Context

The whirlwind of changing state and federal policies, standards, and assessments, and the increasing inequality and deepening poverty, were taking a toll on a district with a low tax base frustrated with and at times infuriated by the outflow of public resources and state funds to suburban districts and charter and private schools. We were a community unsupported even by its own state legislators and governor, who launched an unrelenting attack on urban Indiana school districts and their efficacy. These attacks created a narrative of failure, one which framed the public schools as unable to serve their neediest children. And on the national stage, even the No Child Left Behind Act achievement language became part of the rationale for subverting public dollars to fund private and public charters. The state of Michigan, for example, is the poster child for charters without much state or local governmental oversight, and their record of meeting the needs of historically disenfranchised students is deplorable.

The Funding Challenge

In the fallout of the national recession in 2008, Indiana and many other states began to find new ways to manage their shortfalls. As the economy turned downward, local revenues fell with the drop in property values, and state revenues plummeted with declines in earnings and income. The state of Indiana cut $3.5 million from the Warren District budget, representing a local cut of 3 percent to the district's general fund. In a 2017 report, "A Punishing Decade for School Funding," researchers found investment in K–12 schools sharply declined due to the recession. The report states that even today, state education budgets are not back to where they were before 2008. The researchers found that in 2015, "29 states were still providing less total school funding per student than they were in 2008."[1]

The National Center for Education Statistics report for the last school year, 2016–17,[2] noted that there were substantial variations across the states in the percentages of public school revenues coming from state, local, and federal sources. In twenty-two states, more than half of all revenues came from state governments, while in sixteen states and the District of Columbia, more than half of all revenue came from local governments. In the remaining twelve states, no single revenue source comprised more than half of all revenues. How can we support students without the proper local versus state and federal funding streams?

Indiana has not been immune to the shifting education values occurring throughout the country, whether disguised behind the recession or not.

> State leaders have implemented new grants that provide money to teachers where student achievement is high . . . this is correlated with poverty thus providing millions of dollars to districts that least need the help . . . Indiana leaders implemented a new funding formula in 2014 that shifted money away from a factor called the "complexity index" . . . Over two years, this removed approximately $500 million dollars in funding from high poverty schools and shifted it to districts that serve, on average, wealthier, less-diverse students.[3]

Budgets in Indiana have favored wealthy students over others. Public educators in Indiana have witnessed a deliberate disinformation campaign and the subsequent dismantling and deconstruction of funding for public schools from a front-row seat. We educators and board members have witnessed the steady reallocation of funds to three sources: charters; private schools for urban students; and, most recently, for mostly middle-class families earning $54,000 or more per year. This change in complexity gave the "free and reduced lunch" state funds to suburban districts and the "free" lunch state funds to urban districts. This left fewer resources for students with the most complex needs, eliminating counselors and social workers to support those inside the urban beltway in and around Indianapolis, Fort Wayne, South Bend, and Gary. Indeed, for Warren, it would take the federal grant to bring back the funds needed for innovation, for professional development, and for retaining our high-quality and experienced staff, along with positive behavior intervention and support. It took another local referendum to increase property tax in order to secure the funds to provide our teachers with a competitive professional salary.

The last twenty years have been filled with volatility, uncertainty, complexity, and ambiguity—or VUCA,[4] as coined by the US Army War College at the end of the Cold War. We live in a world that is rapidly changing and increasingly unstable, and it is clear that we can expect our future to be equally unpredictable and challenging. As Warren Bennis and Burt Nanus, authors of the 1985 book *Leaders: Strategies for Taking Charge*,[5] state: "We are moving from a world of problems which demand speed, analysis and elimination of uncertainty to solve—to a world of dilemmas, which demand patience, sensemaking and an engagement with uncertainty." As educational inquirers and practitioners and—perhaps above all else—people, we have struggled to cope with change and uncertainty in our own individual lives—not to mention the tumultuous wave of state activity afflicting the world of education. Only naturally, then, we must look to each other for help and advice.

Reframing the Problem as an Opportunity

That is where the funding challenge lay when I became the assistant superintendent for elementary instruction pre-K to sixth grade and joined the district leadership team in Warren Township:

- The State Department had just announced cuts to local district budgets for the school year.
- In our district, we had Moorhead and Heather Hills, two elementary schools in need of renovation, both centrally located with a good deal of community pride and history.
- The district team was seeking to implement a new set of standards and assessments and had a state mandate to change the teacher evaluation system.
- We had a new state technology requirement that would prove costly to upgrade the aforementioned two schools.

The two schools in need of renovation had a combined teaching staff of 149 (ancillary staff, i.e., cafeteria workers, custodians, etc., not included in this number), a thousand students, and school principals to relocate from our existing eleven elementary schools. Simultaneously, the inequity across the district's schools was rising. Our middle schools were lagging academically and the community was demanding a way to rethink opportunities for an increasingly diverse student body through redistricting and a balanced school calendar for the entire district—this is what destabilization looks like for a school superintendent and her board of education: a number of choices, all of them dramatically affecting all of the district's stakeholders and constituents, none of them easy to make, and none of their potential outcomes predictable.

After much deliberation, in 2009 the district leadership team recommended to the superintendent closing the two aging elementary schools as a budget-cutting measure, therefore reducing the number of elementary schools from eleven to nine. The district team knew that there was capacity for additional students in its middle schools to accommodate a large number of younger students (grade five). We felt that framing the financial shortfall as a possibility and an opportunity to expand the equity of learning opportunities for all students, and not as a budget cut, was the way to go. I argued within the cabinet that this shortfall would be a good time to rebalance and restructure all K–8 schools to better achieve equity of opportunity and access to the highest performing schools, principals, and teachers in the district. After much consideration, the cabinet decided that it would be best to close the two oldest elementary schools that required the most work (capital projects). These buildings were difficult to wire with technology, and one of the schools, Moorhead, was built with cinder block. Both needed extensive renovation and repair.

Moorhead and Heather Hills Elementary Schools

The two buildings we decided to close were the most beloved elementary schools in the district. The Moorhead community fought hard for the continued operation of the school. Prior to its closing, Moorhead had an enrollment of 465 students, kindergarten through five, and had twenty-six teachers and additional ancillary staff. One of the most ethnically diverse schools in the district, Moorhead's student makeup was approximately 2 percent Asian, 43 percent Hispanic, 17 percent Black, and 37 percent White students. Moorhead was above the state average but below the district average in terms of the percentage of students who qualified for free or reduced-price lunches. On average, 43 percent of students in Indiana at the time qualified for free or reduced-price lunch programs, whereas 57 percent of Moorhead Elementary School students did. At the district level, approximately 60 percent of students qualified (data supplied by ProPublica, 2011).[6] The percent of Moorhead students achieving proficiency in math was 77 percent, which was higher than the state average of 76 percent for the 2009–2010 school year. The percent of students achieving in English Language Arts (ELA) was the same as the state average at 76 percent.

The other school, Heather Hills, had student enrollment of 535 students in grades kindergarten through five and thirty-one teachers and additional ancillary staff. It was above both the district and state average for the percentage of students eligible to receive free or reduced-priced lunch, with 78 percent of students in these lunch programs. The school's demographic was 1 percent Asian, 83 percent Black, 2 percent Hispanic, and 14 percent White. The percent of Heather Hills students achieving proficiency in math was 67 percent; ELA was 68 percent—both below the state average.

Matt Barnum's "Five Things We've Learned from a Decade of Research on School Closures"[7] lays out how closures can affect students' academic performance in different cities and states. First, in many places, closures hurt students academically; nationwide, closures appear to slightly lower test scores. Second, the quality of the school that displaced students end up moving to matters greatly. Third, in some cases, other students do slightly worse when their school receives an influx of students from closed schools. Fourth, the long-term effects on future students are unknown.

And fifth, the impact of school closure on communities and students goes beyond academics. Researchers have documented consequences that are not easy to measure. Researchers posit in these studies that 40 percent of students reported that the closure of their school damaged their friendships or relationships with others. Students felt they were stereotyped at their new school. "People label us as bad, stupid, or useless but people don't know what it feels like to be forced out and no one will ever understand the struggles we face every day," one student said. A final point is that school closures disproportionately affect low-income students of color. A national study found that even among low-achieving schools, those with more students of color were more likely to close.

The district team knew it would be hard for these school communities to accept the closures. University of Chicago sociologist Eve L. Ewing noted, "Even when schools are closed as part of an effort to save money, public debate often focuses on another outcome: the pain caused by shuttering a community institution. 'Institutional mourning' is the idea that people mourn institutions the way that they mourn people." She continues, "The way they used this intensely intimate and emotional language to talk about their own reaction to that perceived death is something that happened over and over."[8] After months of tears along with passionate, raw, courageous, sweaty, often heated dialogues and community forums, the community eventually blessed the school closures, ultimately circumventing the dilemma the district faced in light of the state's bleak economic forecast.

The Changes Required and the Results

This left the district leadership with 149 teachers to reassign or replace due to the school closure and retirements. This work was accomplished through a two-pronged approach: HR spent time working on reassignments, while the cabinet worked on the restructuring and placement of students. Along with revising student transportation routes, the cabinet also had to ready the receiving buildings with technology, equipment, and other services that would uniquely separate the space into two distinct school environments: one for elementary-age students and one for middle school students.

With that said, the district team reassigned eight hundred to nine hundred fifth-grade students to the 6–8 buildings: these new schools (environments) became intermediate academies with fifth through sixth students housed upstairs in the middle schools and seventh- to eighth-grade students downstairs. The arrangement had an additional benefit: it extended and deepened the elementary implementation of the district's instructional model, the eight-step process, to be resident in all of the district's middle schools. The incoming sixth-grade students continued an elementary model, which gave them additional time to develop literacy and math skills in a more formal, student-centered, age-appropriate learning setting. And, eventually, another benefit of restructuring emerged: it extended the teaching of reading to all seventh- and eighth-grade students. Middle school teachers became reading teachers as well as content specialists.

This initiative also required the hiring and/or movement of three principals, who with district support helped develop the 5–6 curriculum and designed parent and community communication protocols to be used to introduce incoming families to the larger school community. One of the principals was hired to lead one of the 5–6 intermediate academies at Raymond Park. A year later, results showed that we had made the right decision in placing him there. His school received distinguished state of Indiana I-STEP scores—Indiana academic standards that measure student achievement in mathematics, English, science, and social studies—earning an A+ rating for three consecutive years. Another principal was kind enough to take on Creston Intermediate Academy. He also developed a successful school, with I-STEP scores of A+ in their first year.

There is one more important note here. The district team championed the benefits of a district "Balanced" school calendar. Originally, four of the eleven elementary schools were on a year-round calendar, with four nine-week quarters and three one-week periods over twelve months. This entailed nine-week in-school sessions, then one week off in the fall for parent-teacher conferences, at Thanksgiving break, for Christmas, and for spring break. These same four schools housed and served the highest performing students in the district and were largely Caucasian. In order to maintain both parent and teacher support for the redistricting for equity, we merged the year-round and traditional school calendars into one district calendar: nine-week quarters, two weeks off for all schools. The new calendar preserved an extra month of remediation time for students who needed more support to master the expected skills. During the first week of the break between nine-week quarters, remediation was offered to all students who needed extra help or enrichment. These half day extra sessions especially pleased parents and gave students the opportunity to catch up.

Summary

This chapter provided a description of the headwinds Warren Township Board of Education and our district leadership team had to navigate as we dealt with unplanned and unexpected events and changes in our demographics, community, and state economy. As a district team working with our board and community, we came to a solution: two school closings, redistricting the district, restructuring the elementary and middle school grade levels, and a balanced school calendar that appealed to both existing constituents while increasing equity of access to high quality education and outcomes for our most vulnerable students.

Once we worked through the institutional mourning in our community, we found the acceptance and resolve to move all levels of the district forward to implement a complex, multifaceted solution that we felt would benefit all students, staff, and families. Fortunately, all school-based leadership took up the challenge to invite the transitioning students into their new schools. As we expected, our students continued to thrive in a more challenging and ever-changing curriculum with teachers who also had to make accommodations to provide rigorous and engaging instruction.

Lessons Learned

Clearly, school funding, even in good economic times, is an issue, but school funding when state government is deliberately taking away dollars to support charters and suburban districts with more ability to tax locally is even worse. We, like most of you, would look internally for savings, reaffirm important priorities, and defer buying new buses or reduce capital projects plans in order to save to recruit and retain teachers and needed support services like nurses, counselors, or speech therapists.

But I think what one needs to do is ask: is there a new opportunity we should consider—like a new federal or state grant—or a possible school consolidation effort—like a reconfiguration—that could both save dollars and open up new possibilities for grouping multiage students? Is there a better way to use our existing personnel in special education at the high school level that provides for more in-class support and collaboration than self-contained special education classes?

The search for possibilities and new opportunities begins with the question of what future do we wish to pursue? What future do we envision for our students and staff, and what does that require of us to prepare for their future? What is happening in the larger context of our nation and world that we need to investigate and consider?

Whatever new possibilities might emerge, I have come to believe that you can only build on your current strengths—the positive core of personnel or community assets that relate to the possibilities that you envision. Closing schools in our case afforded us many advantages besides saving money. Shifting our enrollment enabled us to deal with inequity of opportunity and gave us a chance to rebalance our system. The search for possibilities might be limited, but they open up when you consider who is benefiting and who is not. What right cause might we entertain that moves into a new loop? What does the new loop require? Why are we maintaining some old loop practices?

Reflection Questions

1. The obvious questions first: What are your priorities? Which of your professed values are in jeopardy of being compromised? In times of tight budgets and slow growth, identify those values in relation to programs and services for students, families, and staff. Those values should come first.

2. Who is not benefiting from your programming and services? Whose needs are screaming out to you and your team and board of education? How does a cut in funding affect those who are not already benefiting? Who needs to know and become an ally in promoting a new solution?

3. What are your options? Are they truly all on the table for discussion and adjustment? How will you choose a direction for the next year? Next three years? How will you know it's the right choice for now? Who might be brought along for this choice to become your next best asset? What stakeholders do you need to consult internally and externally to obtain their commitment and support before implementation of your selected option? Who else might be affected and how will you provide for them?

4. How will you craft a message that is inclusive of all programs and services and their respective constituencies? Does the message offer a clear statement of direction and implications for others affected and not directly affected? Is it a win-win message or win-loss message? How do you show that you considered all the options?

References

[1] Michael Leachman, Kathleen Masterson, Eric Figueroa. "A Punishing Decade for School Funding," Center on Budget and Policy Priorities, November 29, 2017, https://www.cbpp.org/research/state-budget-and-tax/a-punishing-decade-for-school-funding.

[2] National Center for Education Statistics. "Public School Revenue Sources," last updated April 2020, https://nces.ed.gov/programs/coe/indicator_cma.asp.

[3] Kokomo School Corporation. "The Importance of Equitable Funding in Education," n.d., https://www.kokomoschools.com/our_district/superintendent/superintendentgoals/increase_funding_for_schools_with_the_highest_pove.

[4] Richard H. Mackey Sr.. *Translating Vision into Reality: The Role of the Strategic Leader.* Carlisle Barracks, PA: US Army War College, 1992.

[5] Warren Bennis and Burt Nanus. *Leaders: Strategies for Taking Charge.* New York: HarperCollins, 1985.

[6] ProPublica. "The Opportunity Gap: Is Your State Providing Equal Access to Education?," last updated January 24, 2013, https://projects.propublica.org/schools/.

[7] Matt Barnum. "Five Things We've Learned from a Decade of Research on School Closures," *Chalkbeat*, February 5, 2019, https://www.chalkbeat.org/2019/2/5/21106706/five-things-we-ve-learned-from-a-decade-of-research-on-school-closures.

[8] Eve L. Ewing. *Ghosts in the Schoolyard: Racism and School Closings on Chicago's South Side.* Chicago: University of Chicago Press, 2018.

CHAPTER FOUR

Transforming Teaching and Learning

Dena gave us that context of connecting old with the new. It's not that we're in a same place than we were six years ago with Loop One, and she realizes we're going to be in a different place six years from now, the move to Loop Two. The challenge is balancing the old with new in order to bring about the change for the future, making it seamless. I think of that as being one of her lasting impacts. —Ryan Russell, Assistant Superintendent K–5

The vertigo and what caused it: The failure of most states to adopt the next generation Common Core standards after four years of preparation and implementation locally, placed districts in limbo for over five years waiting for new state standards replacement and adoption, and then another two years to prepare for a new state assessment.

In early September 2012, the board president and I decided to pursue a US Department of Education Race to the Top grant. After six grueling weeks, the district administration and teachers submitted our district's application to the Department of Education. We had no expectation of being awarded the grant, even when we received word that our grant was one of 171 of the original 372 submitted that had moved into the next round of consideration.

Two months later, the cabinet had just finished a brainstorming session in the creative thought gallery at Warren Central High School. The team was aligning our goals for the upcoming year and creating a visual representation of the work moving forward.

I returned to my office from the meeting to organize my thoughts, but my typing was interrupted by an email that popped up. It read: "Congratulations, you have been awarded a Race to the Top grant for $28.5 million." I could not move. I pushed Print . . . got out of my chair . . . went to the printer, and walked to cabinet members' offices. No one had returned from the morning work session at the high school. I had to wait until lunch to share this life-changing opportunity with the team. When I did, we screamed, we danced, and we sang "Celebrate Good Times" by Kool & The Gang.

Warren was one of sixteen school districts from eleven states and Washington, DC, to receive nearly $400 million to support local plans to personalize student learning, improve student achievement and educator effectiveness, close achievement gaps, and prepare every student for college and career readiness.[1] The $28.5 million we received was distributed over four years and we sought and received a fifth-year extension.

Implementation Is a Learning Process

Our celebration was short lived because soon we needed to roll up our sleeves as the implementation work began. We had no idea of the work involved in executing a four-to-five-year grant, including the intricacies of grant stipulations, reporting requirements, and projected timeline deliverables.

Now, the next generation of students in Warren Township, where over 75 percent of kids received either free and reduced lunch, would have a brighter future. Warren was already a district using a continuous improvement process, but now it would be able to provide the resources to ensure its final push to move out of Loop One—only focusing on state assessment scores to comply with state compliance to basic skills—into Loop Two, a blended digital integration and personalized learning focus for students and staff. This moved Warren toward a new trajectory: 2025 and college and career readiness driven by a renewed moral purpose embedded in a culture of civility, order, respect, and a commitment to equity and excellence for all.

As we began this journey, there were four questions that we asked:

1. What impact does innovation have on student learning? What does it look like?
2. What problems(s) are we trying to solve through technology? What's the solution?
3. How will it strengthen teachers' capacity to improve student learning in a blended learning-digital environment?
4. How will the blended learning model coordinate and align into the district framework of continuous improvement?

Two Loops Model

We found and agreed that the Berkana Institute's Two Loops Model was an excellent means to illustrate how our transition from the descending loop or the predominant national model of federal- and state-driven accountability, which I call a scripted basic skills model driven by external accountability metrics to the ascending loop—an inquiry-driven, internally driven accountability model directed by students through a personalizing learning process to better prepare students with twenty-first-century dispositions and critical-thinking skills as they encounter a complex, often chaotic, interdependent world.

Board Resolution and Policy Change

As a district, several lessons came with the implementation of the grant. First and foremost, after the grant was awarded, I asked the board of education to understand that as we transformed from a behavioral linear model of improvement to a more innovative, anytime, anywhere model of learning, it would take time to prepare teachers and students for the next generation of teaching and learning standards. I challenged the board to be patient with the schools as they learned a new pedagogy using instructional tools based on our new technology-based supportive environment. There was a lot on our teachers' plates: the grant; Common Core standards, then the Common Core backlash; the New Indiana College Career Standards replacing CCSS; and the new assessment, I-LEARN—because we didn't use PARCC, the state decided on developing a new assessment.

As we started the transformation to a personalized learning model, I discussed with board members the impact of uncertainty in state policy on our transforming implementation process. We decided to pass a local board resolution that prioritized our new teaching (focused on college and career readiness and increased graduation rates) rather than A–F metrics for test scores that were constantly changing. This passed in the 2012–13 school year as a way to reduce the negative impact of state policy and the ever-changing accountability and assessment systems. With that, the board established the foundation to build on the successes of the district to support the transformation and focus on college and career readiness, personalized learning, and positive behavioral intervention system. The board purposefully created a new narrative for student and teacher success after the state abruptly—and intentionally—pulled out from the Common Core standards. The beginning of the transformation from Loop One to Loop Two was ignited with the new policy.

With my cabinet, I communicated to the board that our goal was to diversify the district educators' innovation teaching and learning options. Our goal was not to increase state test scores but rather to introduce an innovative way of teaching to prepare students for life beyond school—after 2025. We believed this could be accomplished through personalized/customized instruction and individual learning goals for every teacher and child, pre-K to 12.

Guiding Principles

The purpose of Warren Township's new work in Loop Two was to personalize learning through integrated digital content (technology), provide real-time access to student learning data to address individual needs, transform teaching and learning, and create a district-wide positive behavioral support intervention system. We came to define personalized learning as students getting the instruction they need, when they need it. It means teachers need to know how students learn, their current skill level, and dispositions toward learning. This deep level of student knowledge includes knowing why they are learning what they are learning and what they hope to accomplish, how they are finding personal meaning and purposing their own learning, and how they are taking responsibility for it.

As superintendent, I saw our work as the means to carry out the goals assigned to me by the board at the beginning of my term to improve the image of the school district in the community, and, more importantly, to extend the equity of access and opportunity to learn twenty-first-century skills in a one-to-one learning environment. Within six months of assuming my position, the challenge became to personalize and deepen student learning, directly improve student achievement through personalization, improve educator effectiveness, close the achievement gaps, and prepare every student to succeed in college and/or their chosen careers.[2] Educational consultant Anthony Kim presented to our staff a way to move forward with personalized learning at our open day kick off in 2015.

At the end of this chapter, we placed a disclaimer that this work can only be accomplished with a major external influx of state and or federal dollars. We offer our thoughts on how to begin and sustain the transformation to a more personalizing learning platform.

A New Educational Infrastructure

How does a school district digest $28.5 million tied to three major goals, create a new infrastructure to support the innovations, and apply an implementation plan that helps a Loop One district move into a demanding Loop Two innovation cycle? We used the Wallace Foundation's Theory of Action[4] to develop coherence for the many projects we had to accomplish over the four years of the grant. Infrastructure, the classroom, and anytime, anywhere learning is where we consistently put the team's passion and energy to transform our continuous improvement process. The infusion of technology into personalized learning helped create high-quality curriculum. Innovative professional development was the ultimate outcome year one.

Infrastructure was critical if we were serious about access for all students in a personalized learning model. We had to ensure that all buildings had Wi-Fi access points. This was difficult at the beginning, but as we learned more about our buildings' capacity to handle technology, we were able to better outfit them appropriately. We also worked with companies to understand district data storage and what was needed to support and update student data daily. We started to discuss "the cloud" in ways that some of us did not understand; we had to rely on those with that skill set and trust that they knew what we did not.

Our expanded district platform of work included eleven projects, listed below. Each project comprised our developing infrastructure to support our transformative work in Loop Two.

1. Curriculum, Instruction & Formative Assessment (K–12)
2. Personalized Learning System: Online Formative Assessment and Data Dashboard to Track Progress
3. Environment to Support Engaged Learning (Pre-K–12)
4. Extending Time Learning Opportunities
5. Professional Opportunities
6. Grant Implementation
7. Virtual Learning Opportunities
8. Extending Learning Opportunities (ELO)
9. Sports and Media Opportunities
10. PBIS and Culturally Responsive Instruction (Pre-K–12) CORE
11. Parents Are the Core (K–6)

During this time there were a number of innovative accomplishments. We exited the descending, test-focused loop by incorporating the Common Core standards into our curriculum maps and calendars. We also started preparation for the rigorous inquiry for deeper learning and preparations for PARCC assessment as a deliverable of the federal grant. Although the state of Indiana had not made a final decision whether to go with PARCC, Smarter Balanced, or create its own standards-based assessment, we recognized that online assessment was an important component of modern school systems. We incorporated a number of online tools for predictive and diagnostic assessments to tailor instruction for individual students. We believed personalized, data-driven learning was critical to student success and moved to a one-on-one student computer model to achieve that goal. We prioritized a comprehensive network upgrade to support one-on-one teaching and learning in the belief that the future of education will depend on a robust infrastructure.

We now have Common Core teachers and staff that model lessons, conduct data meetings, participate in team teaching, teach intervention, and lead professional development. With the grant, our continuous improvement ascends by shifting our instructional focus to Common Core standards and the commitment to personalized data-driven learning. While there were concerns about the rigor of the upcoming assessments, we believed the ascending loop was the best way to prepare as a comprehensive implementation of CCSS in the classroom through the intersection of instruction and technology.

Initial Implementation: Technology and Personalized Learning

Warren Township wanted to implement personalized learning district-wide while increasing student engagement, collaboration, and self-directed learning. We made many early investments to create classrooms that we hoped would meet our goals. Early implementation actions included creating curriculum units aligned to new Common Core standards; distributing devices (Chromebooks) directly to students in grades 7 through 12 and Chromebook carts to each pre-K through sixth classroom; and renovating high school classrooms and fifth through eighth media centers.

The high school media center had been renovated earlier into a learning environment with critical thought galleries. The thought gallery was a space with white board technology and computers. The premise was to start with an idea or concept on a document and let others build on. It invited participation and collaboration from all involved in solving the problem, concept, or expanding the idea. These spaces, which included modern, practical technology, promoted collaboration and increased teacher-student engagement.

Initially, we constructed our district value statement for personalized learning that spoke for everyone in the learning environment: "We are all learners who deserve personalized learning experiences to become leaders who have the skills to be successful in life and create solutions for a better tomorrow." This statement of belief put us on course for change in our classrooms, which led to a collaborative, engaging, and self-directed learning experience for students, teachers, and principals.

In our first year, we implemented many of these eleven project efforts but were not seeing the impact at the classroom level. We struggled with how to successfully incorporate technology to personalize instruction for student and teachers. While we had a well-thought-out technology rollout plan, we had an immature process for selecting the relevant digital content needed to support personalized learning platforms. We also learned that the Chromebook distribution was manageable at the high school level, but the devices could not withstand the rough and tumble of being mixed into student backpacks. Each computer needed its own carrying case.

We also had not fully articulated or communicated our belief system for personalized learning, including answers to questions such as: What problem(s) are we trying to solve with technology? How will personalized learning fit into our district framework of continuous improvement? What support do teachers need to implement personalized learning? In the beginning, teachers used the individual computers as a reward for completing assignments. We knew that was not transformative or innovative. We needed outside support.

Technology Rollout and Improvements

Throughout the early implementation period, the district modified its operations to effectively manage the distribution and maintenance of devices. To increase the efficiency of distribution, the district integrated the process of distributing four thousand laptops to high school students with the distribution of class schedules at the start of school. The district identified a place to store devices at each school and hired ten staff to clean and service all laptops and tablets each summer. During the school year, students in the Career Center fixed broken screens as part of its computer science and repair course. The lesson learned here was that the turnaround time required to repair and get the laptop back to students was problematic. Eventually, we selected a vendor to insure and replace equipment quickly.

The district had an IT help desk prior to the grant but hired two additional technicians to manage service calls. Unforeseen damage to laptops required the district to rethink its approach to device selection and distribution. There was a high rate of breakage among students in grades seven and eight, mainly due to cracked screens because of the weight of students' books in backpacks. Thus with the next purchase of laptops, we sought a more durable device and added hard-cover cases to prevent unnecessary damage to devices. The district purchased new laptops for the incoming ninth graders in 2015–16 because the original devices were in such poor condition. To determine which model to buy, the district compared battery life and tested the durability of four different models through real-life experiences such as dropping devices on the ground and the weight of books in backpacks. District leaders reported that the new models did not damage as easily as those purchased in the summer of 2013.

Effective integration and management of technology led to increases in student engagement and collaboration in the classroom. Early distribution and training for teachers on using technology in the classroom resulted in a gradual change from using the computer to simplify processes to designing tasks that were more creative and engaged students more fully. Instructional specialists shared comments from teachers throughout the district regarding using technology in the classroom as a teaching tool. One teacher reported that if she did not have technology now, she would be lost. A high school teacher observed, "The past two years have also been a growth period for students as they now see devices as an 'instructional tool,' " rather than a form of entertainment. Students could now conduct research online, write up their results and reports, create multimedia presentations and spreadsheets to track their scores on assessments, and can "virtually visit" anything they were discussing. According to another high school teacher, "Technology has made class more collaborative because if students do not have an answer, they can look it up on their laptop rather than the teacher telling them the answer. The search for answers piques their curiosity."

Contracting for External Support: Educational Elements

As a district leadership team, we spent time researching additional information on personalized learning and its implications for teacher development and instruction. Early in the 2014–15 school year, we brought in consultants from Education Elements, an education consulting company with expertise in personalized learning and digital integration, to ensure that our new innovative initiative was being transformed to its fullest potential. Through the Education Elements's workshops, summits, and direct support, we clarified our vision of personalized learning, revised our belief statements, and communicated those statements widely within the school community. Working with Education Elements marked the operational implementation plan to make the transformation to Loop Two—i.e., transforming the culture of teaching and learning in Warren Township. A comprehensive plan for the district using a blended learning lens to transform a teacher's role in a digital learning environment was the starting point. What we learned is that the district's direct instruction, station-center teaching model had evolved, especially in K–8. While we understood the power of instruction reinforced with supplemental learning stations and centers and individual scripted intervention, these activities had limited rigor and mostly consisted of basic skills needed to pass the state assessment (I-STEP). As a district, we were concerned with raising the academic rigor and depth of knowledge in teaching and learning; we wanted to move away from basic skills. The work was the nexus.

The Education Elements team worked with all divisions of the Warren staff to develop a district blueprint, a roadmap of each school's readiness based on the Education Elements analysis of each school's strategy, design, curriculum and instruction, and support and operations. We landed on the cohort model as our rollout strategy. Using the analogy of a swimming pool, some schools were ready to "dive in," others were "wading in the middle," and still others just wanted to "dip their toes in the water."

Changing Course: The Cohort Model

After our initial start and subsequent examination of our blue-print, we launched blended/personalized learning teams in three phases. Phase one and two, included multiple schools composed a cohort. Cohort-1 were the schools ready for a deep dive as determined by the readiness assessment that Education Elements conducted for us. They identified five schools that they felt were ready to be launched into the initial cohort: one elementary, three intermediate academic (fifth through sixth) and one middle school (seventh through eighth). From a district perspective, Cohort-1 was the catalyst for getting Cohort-2 primed to dive. Cohort-2 was made up of our remaining eight elementary schools and our other two middle schools. The high school by itself was considered Cohort-3 because of its size (with 3600 students). We started with the English Department because it was ready and willing to drive into personalizing platform. The high school was also primed by Cohort 2 middle school students moving on.

The personalized learning blueprint defined instructional strategies used in a blended learning classroom as the Core 4: 1) Targeted and/or small group instruction; 2) Integrated digital content and differentiated path and pace; 3) Student reflection and ownership; and 4) Data-driven decisions. Our lead instructional specialist explained that the trainer model allowed schools to select which of the Core 4 instructional strategy points to focus on initially. "They each selected one of the above Core 4. Most schools selected targeted or small group instruction. We had a couple of other schools that picked student reflection and ownership; one that picked data-driven decision-making, and that was pretty incredible."

The trainer of trainers model provided an area to work

on, while also promoting autonomy and ownership of the innovation. Our lead specialist continued: "There's ownership and there is a guideline—we called them 'guardrails.' Giving them [teachers and schools], like we do with students, voice and choice in the aspects of learning. Within guardrails it's not all over the map; that's the road that we are on." Teachers are then given a timeline, and the district would celebrate their work and widen their goal to coincide with the school-wide initiatives.

The district embedded blended learning within its district framework to better communicate how it would be one of its tools to increase student growth and achievement. As the district's work continued within our theory of action, all leadership teams, including students at all levels, were granted more "voice and choice" in their own professional or personal development to model how blended learning could be used to personalize learning in the classroom. Through these experiences, district leaders recognized that schools had teachers with varying levels of readiness or willingness (based on computer skills) to implement blended learning.

District leaders realized that personalized learning would look different for high schoolers than it would for elementary or middle schoolers. All district schools began with a discovery phase where staff observed outside district blended learning schools and explored an online playlist of digital resources, while teachers began to experiment with new practices in the classroom. The five schools in Cohort-1 implemented blended learning in their classrooms in January 2016. The remaining schools, including the high school, spent more time in the discovery phase before beginning implementation in the 2016–17 school year.

Using Digital Content for Personalized Learning

Personalized learning is a teaching methodology that adapts and responds to each student's ability, level, learning style, interests, and other unique needs. That kind of flexibility requires technology—lots of it. We purchased thirteen thousand Chromebooks for our classrooms and rushed to distribute them to schools. Simple, right? We deployed computers with limited digital content to comply with grant deliverables and to support our continuous improvement process for enrichment, practice, and remediation. Due to the limited digital content options available at the time, we mostly left it up to teachers to figure out, with limited online resources like Kahn Academy or libraries. Because we valued teachers' interests and expertise, we had to rethink our continuous improvement process and how we would assess learning with limited digital content. The district had to revise its approach in vetting online digital content and vendors to ensure that teachers and students gained necessary information to improve learning and personalize instruction.

In 2013, the district had created three-week assessment units that included pre-post unit assessments aligned with the Common Core standards. The district learned from teachers that these assessments took an inordinate amount of time to complete and were not allowing time for deeper learning, critical thinking, and collaboration during class. To address these concerns, the district leaders and teachers created nine-week instructional units with a culminating performance task. This task was designed for students to apply what they have learned to a "real-world" task and required an in-depth understanding of what they had learned through peer collaboration in order to complete the task.

Basic digital content had been integrated into classrooms since devices were first distributed system-wide in a somewhat limited scope in 2013, giving teachers initial access to student learning tools and increasing the availability of real-time data. Having multiple online tools to explore allowed teachers to set goals about what students should know and learn. Monitoring student progress using online assessments built into the tool kit was now part of the process. One elementary school teacher noted digital content had "transformed the job because I can pull the data in two minutes and I can address the feedback and make immediate changes to the day's lesson."

Teachers noted that using these data points was integral to the formation of small groups for targeted instruction. Students appreciated the immediate feedback from using some of the tools. To have a more intentional process for identifying digital content that is the right "fit" for the district, the district tasked an existing staff member with the responsibility of vetting digital content and working with vendors. The district was still developing the specifics of the process but had discussed vetting content two times per year and assessing the cost, systems needed to support the content, and licensing terms before making final decisions.

The Core 4 and Professional Development

During the fourth year of the transformation implementation plan, the district continued to find ways to go deeper in its application of blended learning. One of the Core 4 strategies inherent to the district's approach in achieving a more system-ic scaling of blended learning was supporting teachers' use of new instructional practices through professional development and coaches. According to an elementary school teacher in the district, "Some of the best professional development has been meeting with similar grade level teachers at other schools."

Supporting new instructional practices through professional development and our instructional specialists was key in fundamentally changing how students would learn. Initially, much of the training focused on revised curriculum, mapping calendars, and using technology, but in 2015, the focus shifted to using blended learning practices to personalize student learning based on the Core 4. To support teachers as they adjusted to the new strategy, training focused on mastering the use of targeted and small group instruction (research on station-teaching by Marilyn Friend[3] informs this type of instruction—direct instruction, small group application, and individualize digital content in a ninety-minute block) then beginning to use the other three components. Key to helping teachers better understand how to use blended learning to personalize instruction was the leaders redesigning their professional development to model how a personalized learning classroom should function. For example, professional development must include sixty minutes of collaborative time that is "completely personalized" in that the teachers choose what they work on and want to know more about.

Teachers reported that the collaboration time helped as they experimented with new strategies; they used the time to reflect on what was working—and what was not. Most schools have shifted away from whole-group staff meetings to just-in-time approaches focused on transformation skill development.

CORE Social and Emotional Development

Blended learning training has been complemented by the district's approach to classroom management in its Positive Behavior Interventions and Supports (PBIS) program using Civility, Order, Respect, and Excellence (CORE), and in 2014, the district began training teachers on using these strategies. With grant funds, we had an outside expert guide us through a yearlong exercise aimed at understanding school culture and developing strategies based on each school's student population and data. By 2015, CORE had been fully implemented and district staff felt that everyone had the same expectations for behavior in the classroom and a "common language." District staff believe these strategies have led to a positive change in students' behavior and a decrease in suspensions and expulsions in 2014–15.

Prescribing to Coaching

In addition to personalizing professional development, district leaders felt that regular feedback was a necessary component of teacher support as they began using new instructional practices. The district significantly restructured the purpose of existing coaching practices to align with the focus on blended learning and to ensure that these positions could be sustained post-grant. In the first year of the grant, coaches worked with teachers on curriculum content, and classroom teachers served as e-learning mentors to support the integration of new laptops and tablets. In 2015, the literacy coach position, previously focused on supporting teachers in the area of language art and basic reading instruction, was replaced by the instructional specialist position. This eliminated outdated e-learning positions.

The instructional specialist position was designed to focus on instructional practices rather than content. Staff had to apply for the position, and some former literacy coaches were selected. Instructional specialists participated in separate professional development with external organizations on how to effectively coach and support the blended learning model. Instructional specialists reported that the training was transformative and helped them "understand [that] their job was to help teachers think reflectively versus providing all the answers." Moreover, instructional specialists found that working collaboratively with one another helped them learn more about what they can do to support teachers in using blended learning and transforming teaching and learning. To aid in the collaborative process among instructional specialists, the district created three district-wide learning coordinators to ensure a systematic approach to professional development and coaching.

With Educational Elements support, we created an agreement about personalized learning as a district, an implementation plan, and better online and offline assessment that provide real-time data regarding student performance. We were excited about the rollout plan and how it built teachers' capacity to improve student outcomes and learning. We improved the technology too—the Chromebooks we now use are more durable. They can withstand the pressure and weight of books in backpacks and the routine habits of teens. Teachers now have access to data in real time and can adjust instruction by the minute, hour, day. For the first time during the grant period, I believed we had found the sweet spot for what technological engagement with students should look like in the future.

Self-Assessment and Adjustment

How do nineteen schools successfully implement a Loop Two transformation directed from the district offices to each principal's office and to each teacher's classroom? How do students and their parents come to know and accept these new standards and expectations for learning? We wanted to stretch teacher monitoring of student data district-wide through technology-supported assessments. Through the Request for Proposals (RFP) process, we selected 5-Star Technology, a novice learning management company that later became known as PIVOT, which delivered a system created to perform assessments. We piloted PIVOT's teacher evaluated system with principals and pushed intensive use in actual classrooms to see if the system was effective. We found that it failed to deliver online assessments in a timely manner. PIVOT never met its promise. Implementation is a learning process.

We have placed our second end of the year report in Appendix B in order to illustrate how we held ourselves accountable in our progress toward our intended goals. We felt compelled to share this report as a way to illustrate how progress reports need to be framed during the onboarding process for the board, community, and staff to best encourage a new mindset and the practices required in a personalized learning environment. With five years of changes in our state standards and assessment, we needed a new way of reporting our work and its outcomes to our many publics. Some highlights we would underscore are:

(1) 97 percent of the first cohort of teachers agreed that they were able to provide more differentiated instruction with the personalized learning system;

(2) 80 percent of cohort teachers agreed that students were

more engaged;

(3) 50 percent of students felt school was personalized to what they liked and needed;

(4) Fifth through sixth academies and seventh through eighth middle school were more likely to use small group instruction than ever before;

(5) 88 percent of the cohort teachers were competent in blended learning approaches.

Asked if we could have started over, would we? No. The federal grant has afforded the district the opportunity to take some risks, develop talent, suffer through the "implementation dip" suggested by Michael Fullan (the leading change authority in education) and learn valuable lessons. We have learned that our district team, teachers, and students are resilient when it comes to continuous improvement. We always found a way to get better even when it was messy. We seldom use the word "change"; we now call it "iteration." In a blended learning environment, learning is fluid. I hope that our district will grow and support other districts as they continue to fully transition into personalized learning.

After four years of personalized learning, two of the instructional specialists offered this view:

> We would say probably 95 percent of our staff has been willing to take the risks required to jump into personalized learning. Teachers were willing to try it out. They were willing to make mistakes in front of their administrators and admit, "I tried this. It didn't go well. So, therefore, we are going to try this in a different way.

That really speaks volumes, when you have staff members willing to put themselves out. The district is a safe place where teachers can continue develop their craft because of our leadership commitment to trust and respect their knowledge and insights into how they cultivate their agency. They're willing to try new instructional strategies and to make adjustments as they learn because there wasn't one right way to do almost anything, and I think that's what teachers always want. Iteration is the key to implementation of any complex innovation.

Final Reflection

Throughout this book, we have been emphasizing that continuous learning is fundamental to our district's mission to prepare students and our teachers for the future of work. According to Heather E.McGowan,[5] the global pandemic has required an accelerated pace of changing and embracing digital technology. It has required "a focus on culture enabling the organization to nimbly pivot team operations to enable large scale remote working." She goes on to claim we believe that schools find their purpose in their people; culture if the backbone of resilient districts; work and leadership reconfigure around their people; and humanity unites to support everyone in this time of great moral challenges. Fortunately, we have had in Warren Township a six-year period to prepare for this disruptive season of uncertainly. We created a hybrid model without even knowing that this time would come upon us nationally.

As I reflect on the district and its resilience, I am convinced our teachers and principals have an open mindset and a moral commitment to increasing student access to quality instruction to ensure equity of opportunity.

Disclaimer

Clearly not many districts will have access to such a large influx of cash to create the transformative loop we were able to in such a short time frame. However, we do hope that other districts can develop a personalized learning mindset. It is the necessary first step of any transformative innovation to come to understand what needs to change. What are your district's assumptions about teaching, learning, and curriculum and instructional control? We believe the questions above, when answered in each district context, are a good starting point for your own platform.

What about the dollars for all the training and partnerships with an external entity that can help facilitate the development of local talent to sustain the transformation? I argue that combining Title II, professional development dollars, and STEM or E-Learning grants are a good start to fund your efforts. Some other possibilities?

- Finding partnerships and searching for school districts with federal or state dollars seeking pilots for their project work.
- Seeking out universities with large federal or state contracts that mesh with your vision of the future.
- A partnership with a private for-profit technology or consulting group might leverage your search for additional state or federal projects.
- Finally, local community solicitation for dollars for specialized tasks might generate some income to support your transition to a personalized learning instructional environment and modern technology.

I encourage you to consider these options if a one-to-one or anytime, anywhere learning path is part of the vision for your district. The Warren plan had eleven separate but related components and three major goals. Take look at the table in this chapter to help flesh out the dimensions of your work.

Lessons Learned

- A major and fundamental change like integrating digital content into classrooms through technology requires a full year of engagement from all stakeholders.
- Technology use with students and safety on the Internet requires policy and training.
- Do you know the extent of reliable Internet access in your students' homes? If students do not have access to reliable Internet, one possible solution might be to use buses in neighborhoods as hot spots to facilitate connection.
- Our administrators reported that during the COVID pandemic, our teachers were better prepared to provide in-school, at-home, and hybrid learning to all of our students because of our investment in digital learning.
- Create a teacher team to evaluate and pilot testing relevant digital content before purchasing and installation.
- Seek out a consulting team with deep knowledge and demonstrated expertise if none is available locally.
- Technology implementation requires ongoing and annual review and study before continuing or expanding your district investment so be clear about purpose and use and consider student as well as teacher feedback.

Reflection Questions

Discovering a transformative mindset and designing your own transformative process are the first two steps in moving into the future. We wanted our staff to find the research and the scholarship to help us as a district to evolve from a compliance-standards-based orientation driven by external accountability pressure (Loop One) to personalized learning driven by depth of knowledge using technology and integrated digital content (Loop Two). The district located its positive core of teachers and school-based leaders to build an implementation process that embraces error and iterative changes and improvement over time.

Here are some questions for your deliberations with your own district team or colleagues:

1. Can you describe the mindset that drives teaching and learning today in your school district and some individual schools?
2. Can your team generate the next generation of teaching and learning you believe should be your North Star? Does the Two Loops Model work for you? How would best describe or model it for staff?
3. Can you identify the positive core of talent by name, position, and place in your district and key community partners who enable you to move forward in your schools and community?
4. What prompts might you use to start the conversation? What would you advocate for?
5. Clearly an inventory of talent needs to come first but a close second is what other key capacity—curricular, instructional, technology infrastructure, teacher capacity and learning, should be prioritized.

6. What framework can your district use as a template to drive teacher support and personalized student learning? How will you support teachers in their learning of personalized learning techniques for themselves and their students?

7. How do you engage your parents and community in this transformative work?

What messages can you send and what requests can you make of others to facilitate the new work of teachers, students, and parents? What new roles do each play?

References

1   US Department of Education. "Education Department Announces 16 Winners of Race to the Top-District Competition," December 11, 2012, https://www.ed.gov/news/press-releases/education-department-announces-16-winners-race-top-district-competition.

2   Anthony Kim. *Personalized Learning Playbook*. San Carlos, CA: Education Elements, 2015.

3   Marilyn Friend. *Special Education: 5ᵗʰ Edition Contemporary Perspectives for School Professionals*. 5th Edition. New York: Pearson Education, 2018.

4   The Wallace Foundation. Central Office Transformation Toolkit: Strengthening School District Central Offices in Service of Improved Teaching and Learning, 2013, https://www.wallacefoundation.org/knowledge-center/Documents/Central-Office-Transformation-Toolkit.pdf.

5   Heather E. McGowan. "How the Coronavirus Pandemic Is Accelerating the Future of Work," March 23, 2020, *Forbes*, https://www.forbes.com/sites/heathermcgowan/2020/03/23/the-coronavirus-pandemic-accelerates-the-future-of-work-and-provides-opportunity/?sh=3bc1bb0c317f. David Green and Heather E. McGowan, "How COVID-19 Is Acting As a Catalyst to Accelerate the Future of Work," May 26, 2020, in *Digital HR Leaders Podcast*, https://www.myhrfuture.com/digital-hr-leaders-podcast/2020/5/26/how-covid-19-is-acting-as-a-catalyst-to-accelerate-the-future-of-work.

CHAPTER FIVE

A Human Capacity Paradigm Driving a District Framework

Why do we educate our kids? Is the purpose of education to supply a capitalistic and materialistic economy with new foot soldiers educated enough to complete tasks effectively and keep industry competitive, but not so educated as to question predominant paradigms? The purpose of education should be revisited. In a world focused on a utilitarian perspective on education, education ought to be first a humanistic endeavor. —David Giles, et al.[1]

The vertigo statement and what caused it: the tension that exists between educators and the larger employment community's expectations for the purpose of education is one that changes about every generation or two—transitioning from an industrial society to knowledge society largely through AI and technology. Education is for life and to create a civil society not just for a job!

"Education ought to be first a humanistic endeavor." This statement requires more elaboration and discussion. So we went into some recent literature on reengineering business and not-for-profit organizations and came away with a portfolio of Carol Sanford's scholarship from 2017, 2018, and 2020.[2, 3, 4] We interviewed five superintendents, two from Florida county districts, Mississippi, Washington State, and finally, Warren Township in Indiana to inquire about the efficacy of Sanford's work as a leadership mindset to guide educators' preparation of students for the future. I tried to operationalize that mindset within our district framework and core values that Sanford sees as an appropriate district development plan. She calls for every organization or nonprofit to have development plan for human development. Let us come to know more about Sanford's work and how it might guide educational leadership into a new narrative of education.

Predominant Paradigms

The paradigms that have historically driven the narrative of schooling lie in machine/behavioral and, more recently, information or cybernetics/artificial intelligence narratives. The first focused on standardization, replication, and scaling up efficiencies across the enterprise—from manufacturing to schooling to markets. The second paradigm portrays the mind as an organism. Both machine and organism metaphors are goal directed and use information as feedback to derive "from immediately preceding behaviors." These theories "assume people are controlled by outside forces that immediately precede their actions. People are not independent agents" (Sanford, 2018, 54).

Many argue the way humans change is through feedback provided by experts who observe and critique their practice according to prescribed protocols and the social norms and incentives available within the control of designated agents. There is another way that people change and influence the way they will behave in the future without forcing compliance or substituting praise or punishment that reduces their contributions and novel solutions that persist as a problem of practice. That answer lies in the alternative paradigm.

An Alternative Paradigm: A Development Model of Human Potential

In her book *No More Feedback: Cultivate Consciousness at Work*, Sanford offers a human potential paradigm to guide changes in self and others. This is a "human-centered" view of the world "concerned with human needs and expression; with an emphasis on emotional intelligence and experiential transformation" (50). The next step on the ladder of the paradigm is "knowing life is nested in wholes, each alive, each uniquely expressing and evolving its potential; focus on working developmentally and action modally for systemic reciprocity" (ibid.).

Sanford's three-dimensional developmental model is based upon three core human capacities, where each dimension of human capacity lies on a continuum from external control to internal control, from a focus on self to a focus on the consideration of others. Her three dimensions are:

Locus of Control

Personal Agency

Scope of Considering Others

What is distinct about Sanford's work is how she wraps it into a paradigm or three-dimensional mental model that is inclusive of others. Consideration of others is a significant dimension in that social context offers each of us a sense of place and circumstance beyond ourselves. These three dimensions are always situated in one of three contexts for our purposes—family, school, community—and their corresponding cultures, each with their own norms and expectations that shape individual and collective behavior.

Locus of Control—the degree to which we experience and exercise control over our own lives; particularly on the direction of our self-development and our resilience to adversity. Scope of Considering Others relates to what we take into account including how our actions and endeavors impact other individuals and groups or entire living systems. The difference lies between a self-centered focus on oneself alone and a system actualizing focus on evolving a larger whole—marriage, family, organization, community, industry, ecosystem, planet—in order to create beneficial changes. Source of Agency refers to where we find authority for our initiative and/or actions. It may rely exclusively on the authority of others to direct us or we may have within ourselves the will to initiate action and follow-through with self-directed efforts. The more we are able to direct ourselves, the better our capability to connect to larger systems and help actualize them (22, 24).

Each of these three capacities are locate on a spectrum. Locus of Control moves from external, to seeing our lives determined by others, to internal, taking accountability for what we exercise in terms of outcomes and level of direction. We usually move backward and forward with a tendency toward one or the other by the time we reach adulthood.

Scope of Considering Others signifies gaining a sense of perspective on the internal and external events of our lives. When we consider only ourselves (internal considering), every situation we encounter is all about us. Bruce Barnett noted in personal communication with the author that "the current COVID-19 virus pandemic is another good example of people considering themselves before others by stockpiling far more items than they need to live (meat, dairy products, toilet paper), without considering the needs of other people. Brings back memories of the gasoline crisis in the 1970s."[5] Or preparation when a hurricane or tornado threatens.

On the other hand, if we are sensitive to others in our world and to other forms of life, we have developed a degree of external considering. Like other capacities, we can be at either end of the spectrum and anywhere in between and may be more or less able to be where we want to be all of the time. None of us has constancy on the continuum but again, favor a tendency toward one end or the other.

Source of Agency is also fluid but tends to be directed by beliefs we hold about the world and our roles in it. But especially who has power or influence over us. When we believe we live in an authoritarian world, we often wait for others to activate, direct, give permission, or stop us. But as we become driven internally and come to believe that the world is ours to shape, we begin to move toward a life devoted to stepping up and making a difference. We develop personal agency, or the courage to demand more of ourselves and respond to internal calls that connect us to powerful opportunities. This source is not constant but moves on a continuum from self-centered to systems actualizing. Sanford closes her description of the three capacities by warning,

> without conscious development, these three core capacities may stay nascent our entire lives, diminishing us and limiting the contributions we can make. But if we are willing to develop them by ourselves or with organizations and communities, we may be astounded by how much we can grow and how fully ourselves we can become. The challenge is to avoid the practices and systems that steer us toward a smaller perspective and set of pursuits (24).

She argues these capacities are innate in all people but few institutional roles are designed to develop them. She offers five compelling reasons for the context that controls professional practice across the social roles of attorneys, teachers, doctors, politicians, family, friends, and agencies. We added a sixth: a political discourse. They are presented in short form below:

(1) We are all culturally dependent—there is a dominative pattern of implicit agreements as to how we interpret and make sense of those events. It is hard to go against the grain and if one does, they are threatened and ostracized by groups of people who one looks up to;

(2) There is no process that encourages questioning the assumptions inherent in the dominant messages about why things are the way they are. We are taught these

normative messages our whole lives, first within our families, then schools, by employers, community interactions, police, and social groups; we advocate a critical curriculum approach that starts with skepticism first, critical thinking, and finally, problematization.

(3) The human brain seeks and is drawn to the familiar—naturally, we fear change, or are certainly ambivalent about it, and our brains issue alerts that trigger fear when confronted with unknown events and circumstances, especially when they are not processed to help us deal with what the changes means until after they are implemented;

(4) Few actors in any creative field have access to resource persons in their communities of practice that can help them respond constructively to change (Education Elements served that function for us);

(5) Most of us in any creative field do not have access to the technologies, vocabularies, frameworks, and ways of engaging others needed to develop our highest capacities. Simply, few can succeed without a well-tested and validated model of practice and the training to implement it themselves (16–18);

(6) Finally, we add the toxic circumstances of a nation polarized by nationalism, neoliberalism, and economic inequity where the current political discourse is filled with distraction, disruption, distortion, and lastly, disinformation, which affects people's ability to sort truth from falsehoods. It all deteriorates social trust and erodes our democratic institutions. Time to rediscover and rethink our democracy, starting with asking why these conditions, which impact educational practices and student learning, exist.

Sanford offers educators a new paradigm of living systems and human capacity as a way to rethink not only our purposes, as Giles suggests, but operationally how to do it by eliminating what she calls the toxic practices that hinder the development of human potential and creativity of students, teachers, and school-based leaders. It starts with Why do we do what we do?

Preparing for 2032–33

Do educational institutions in America prepare our children and youth today for the new global landscape and an uncertain future? If changes are in order, how do we go about changing the preparation mindset to embrace and implement them?

In a long-term Gallup study (2018)[6] of management across thirty years of global workplace tracking that engaged millions of in-depth interviews in 155 countries, researchers found that the world's biggest short-term (five to ten years) challenges are declining economic dynamism and productivity. The problem, they also concluded, could not by fixed by lean management or by GE's Jack Welsh's Six Sigma strategies that helped in the past. This time, the defects do not lie in process failures but in the failure to maximize human potential and creativity. The solution, Gallup's Jim Clifton and Jim Harter argue in their book, *It's the Manager*,[7] lies in aligning the practice of management with the new will of the world's workers. Both the American and global dream has changed. What the whole world wants now is a good job. Clifton and Harter argued this is the new will of the world and everything will change when organizations respond to that will. The changing demands of the workforce, in Clifton and Harter's opinion, are presented below in short form. (Our thoughts from a positive strengths–

based perspective are added in italics.)

Past	*Future*
My Paycheck	My Purpose
My Satisfaction	My Development/Learning
My Boss	My Coach/*Peer/Resources*
My Annual Review	My Ongoing Conversations
My Weakness	My Strengths/*Aspirations*
My Job	My Life/*Well-being*

We provide some data here from the Tarrant To & Through (T3) Partnership[8] to illustrate the need for human talent recruitment and the mentoring of nonpredictable minority high schools of color to meet the needs of the workforce for the future. Researchers found that in the Dallas metro area, "By 2036, 71% of jobs in Texas will require a postsecondary credential. But only 32% of high school graduates earn a postsecondary credential within six years of graduating from high school." When compared with Texas's twelve peer states—as Texas competes with them for business expansions and talent—it places last in the population percentage with a postsecondary credential. The pipeline of schools that feed postsecondary institutions and programs desperately needs help. Only 30 percent of Texas fourth graders read at grade level, which also puts the state last among its peers. Not surprisingly, too few Texas students graduate high school prepared for either postsecondary education or the workforce.

What about your state and district's preparedness to provide the human talent they both need to compete locally and globally?

The questions we ask are: How do we change the narrative of schooling that key power brokers and the media historically have promoted? This question requires a discussion about change: How does anyone change anyone else or simply do people change themselves? How do we balance institutional responsibility with individual responsibility to come to know and act appropriately within new norms and expectations of the learning enterprise? What is the new will in modern society?

To help with those question then and today, we have followed the lectures of Ken Robinson.[9] Robinson suggested that education is taking students into a future that is unknown while neglecting the most important human capacity as a distinct part of the curriculum, that is, identifying and supporting the students' innate capacity to create. In his view creativity is as important as literacy today. His fear is that we grow children out of creativity (Sanford's argument too). Our children come to us as diverse, dynamic, and distinct, intelligent human beings, but educators often make very poor use of their talents and in fact dislocate them from their talents. The fundamental structure that needs innovation must move from an educational system focused on linearity, conformity, and batch processing of students through a curriculum of grade level standards tied to the college curriculum.

Emiliana Vegas and Rebecca Winthrop wrote for the Brookings Institution's educational research arm that we must move beyond opening schools during COVID-19 to recognizing the opportunity the pandemic offers. "Public recognition of the essential caretaking role of schools play in society has skyrocketed . . . as communities struggle to take care of their vulnerable children and youth, decision-makers are having to devise new mechanisms for delivering essential services from food to education to health care. They foresee a leapfrog moment for innovation combined with growing inequality and public support, and new educational allies from parents to social welfare organizations coming together to support student learning like never before."[10] Leveraging that support while focused on creating the conditions for an instructional core that offers students the opportunity to be the architects of their own learning through advanced technologies is the centerpiece of their recommendations. COVID-19 has also reminded parents/communities of the inherent value of public schools—nothing else works if the schools aren't there for members of the community.

Finally, our country and business partners demand graduates who are globally aware, financially literate, and who, as Paul Tough says, "have grit, curiosity, persistence, resilience, self-confidence, the ability to influence others and accept feedback from adults and peers which all lead to that most valuable career traits: Character."[11] Character is created by encountering and overcoming failure in this new day—and doing it in the company of your peers who are often better or stronger than you in the classroom. This, then—a focus on practical and team building skills, on real-world applications, on critical thinking—is what our schools needed to emphasize, and this is what was established and agreed upon during the district's town hall meeting.

A New District Framework for 2025 (or 2032–33): The Warren Response

Within my first six months as superintendent, we introduced a moral purpose to guide teachers toward preparing all students for life after school. It was "to be self-directed learners who are literate, creative, civic-minded citizens who do meaningful and productive work in school and life beyond school."[2] As superintendent, I was always promoting to the board of education and my district's and school leadership teams that we were engaged in creating a future for "2025," not the following year. The questions we asked were: What will the world be like for our students entering kindergarten in 2012, who would graduate in 2025? Or today, those who would graduate in 2033? Or retire in 2055, as Kenneth suggested: What is our responsibility to this generation of students growing up in a time where knowledge is dredged up in highly connected social media networks? What role does social media play in this new real-time information age? Do we teach students about the danger of social media platforms and their willingness to promote false narratives without evidence? Should we consider what students will need to know by the time they graduate from school in this ever-changing and unpredictable era? What will it mean to be a productive citizen? What does the workforce require of the new technological society?

We no longer needed graduates who could memorize facts or believe that every answer is found in a book. We no longer needed an educational system that taught students to memorize, regurgitate, and dump information; this was the movement from a Loop One to a Loop Two mindset. No longer do we need a system of accountability-based, vendor-franchised, high-stakes testing.

From 2014 through 2020, Warren transitioned to a student-centered, personalized learning transformative system. Warren's district and school leaders became the resource finders and linkers seeking out illuminators who could help model what others have learned about personalized learning and self-organization at the school and classroom levels. These same illuminators connect within the district to other innovators nationally, so that schools at each level of the pool (1, 2, or 3) learn how different levels and transitions work best for teachers and students. As each school adapts its program regularities (schedules, supports, and resources), it allows for more self-organization and evolving individual student and adult learning.

COR Becomes CORE

The Warren story is an illustration of a district that came to embrace a vision of personalized learning, which was the impetus of our move from Loop One to Loop Two. The spring before I was about to step into the superintendent's office, I traveled to New York with my husband to visit the principal and mentor of two urban high schools on Long Island. He shared how his high schools run on a simple philosophy called COR, Latin for heart. Civility, order, respect. He told us the school staff expected all students to go to college. They were driven by a college prep curriculum, in spite of having diverse and needy populations. He believed they needed a clear purpose and disciplined structure that reinforced the need for interdependence as well as individual commitments to the goals of the school. COR provided that for his staff and the student bodies of the two schools—a combination of college readiness and basic educational values.

As we left New York, we were struck by the implications of that conversation. We felt COR could bring some clarity to Warren's social curriculum and character development K–12. Later that summer, the board set goals for me as the new superintendent that included better public awareness of the school system and a commitment to increase the well-being of the community as a whole. I thought COR, as we would define it, should also include statements about our continuous pursuit of equity of opportunity and excellence for all students. I suggested adding an E for equity and excellence.[2] We introduced the CORE belief system to all district staff at the opening of schools in fall 2012.

Working with a consultant supported with funds from grants, we selected a team of teachers, counselors, and principals and asked them to develop a behavioral support matrix to incorporate the CORE concept in their school improvement plan. Each building was encouraged to build their own response to CORE through PBIS by school. Each school also graphically depicted their own interpretation and application of CORE, posting the vision, purpose, core values, and mission statements across their entrances and hallways. Each school received a small grant to uniquely communicate their school's CORE matrix through an age-appropriate graphic design.

The Warren Framework

As Spillane, et al.; the Wallace Foundation; Anderson and Young; and Burrello, et al.,[12] have proposed, district framework is the translation of a moral purpose and a set of core values into a guiding set of principles that encompass the elements of our district framework for the board of education that placed CORE front and center. In addition to those two elements, Burrello, et al., suggest a framework should include a description of the strategy for improvement. They selected a positive strengths–based change strategy embedded in the work of David L. Cooperrider and Diana Whitney and their colleagues,[13] whose scholarship and practice is described as appreciative inquiry. The other elements Burrello, et al., included are relational leadership and generative learning and capacity building, which are situated within an internal accountability set of metrics and are responsive to external accountability demands. The appreciative organizing diagram illustrating these six elements is depicted in Figure 1, page 111.

This positive strengths–based framework included the draft of our district's purpose statement. These goals were tied to a set of parameters that guided decision-making in pursuit of our purpose statement. The Warren framework, with its constituent parts, is depicted below.

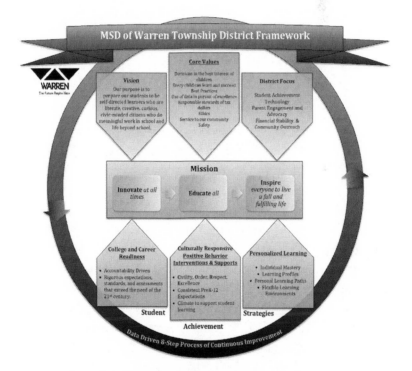

Figure 2: Warren Township District Framework

The framework itself consists of five elements embedded in the districts' continuous improvement model of plan, do, check, and act. The elements are: 1) Vision and Purpose; 2)

Core Values; 3) District Focus; 4) Mission; and 5) Goals. Note that purpose drives goal settings and action in a concrete and less abstract way than most district vision statements, from the board to the classroom. The core values establish the parameters of action and the pursuit of district goals to serve as a means of preventing distraction from the driving purpose of district intent. The district focus is a restatement of the board goals clearly identified for all to see and understand. The mission serves as the rallying cry of the district's chief resource—its people—to innovate constantly—to educate all to high levels—and to inspire each and every one to lead a rich and fulfilling life—*purpose* again is emphasized here.

New District Framework Results: Using Data

This framework concludes with restatements of the district focus and the three outcomes that drove action and support to every level of the district support system. My district leadership team searched for a process to link district leadership action and support that reached into the classroom to improve teaching and learning. We translated the district focus from top administration to each level of leadership, which is depicted in figure 3—the Wallace framework that tracks district-level support to the classroom and student success.

What we found is that while a twenty-first-century purpose, vision, and core value is at the heart of building goals in Warren, our own DNA is more importantly alive and well in the hearts and minds of the leadership and the school staff. It all starts with an open mindset that my team had, then brought to our dialogue. My assistant superintendent, now my successor, Dr. Tim Hanson, noted: " 'The Warren Way' starts with an innovative mindset. We have an innovative spirit that I think it goes hand in hand with the continuous improvement process that excellence is our goal, not perfection. It's hard work." His assistant superintendent observed: "None of us can predict what 'ready' means. It was just trying to find some of those things that would really help them be successful no matter what our world is going to be like in 2025."

My team of instructional specialists and principals searched for a process to help describe the flow of actions from students to the district office, and we found the Wallace Foundation's toolkit helped to link central office actions to classrooms of teachers and students by school (see Honig). We were able to identify the desired student outcomes within each of the three initiatives in the district framework, and then detail what we wanted to see in each classroom and each school. This allowed district leaders to formulate and communicate a district response to support movement toward specific desired student outcomes. We offer below one example of a specific outcome for CORE implementation. Appendix A features the entire list of desired outcomes in terms of each strategic initiative; coherence can be traced from the top down in the district's thinking and action.

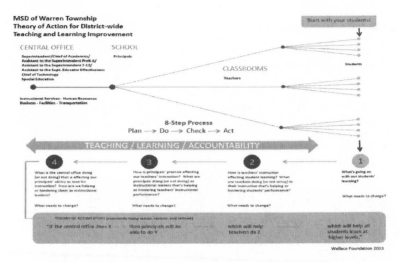

Figure 3 The Wallace Workflow from Central Office to Students

As you review the Wallace Foundation's district level planning document above, check out the largest frame—Central Office, School, Classrooms, Students—and note it starts with student need. Then observe the flow below—if the central office does 4, then principals will be able to do 3, which will help teachers do 2, which will in turn help all students learn at higher levels 1. A snapshot of this level is displayed here in tabular form. The team established ten student outcomes and produced nine other examples. The completed table has been placed in Appendix A.

Sample page of APPENDIX A: 21st Century Readiness Skills

Below is the goal outcome for CORE:

1. Student will model civility, order, respect, and excellence.		
Teachers will:	**Building Administrators will:**	**District Office Admin. will:**
• Model • **Build relationships** • Develop class plans (aligned to Building plans) • Build relationships • Teach CORE plans • Analyze data for trends constantly • Monitor reactions/ decisions • Speak to students as if they believe they all belong here	• Share data with staff • Be consistent with plan and implementations • Model for teachers and students • Give school-wide staff recognition • **Support the plan** • Work with parents • Lead communication • Provide PD • Discipline data meetings as needed	• Provide data • Provide money • **Communicate with all stakeholders on data and training** • Give technical support • Provide training • Recognize building administration • Revise R&R handbook • Coordinate with PBIS

One of the clearest examples of how the district framework helps the district compete with its peer districts can be seen in the use of the framework by the district's human resources department. Our director stated it helped with recruiting teachers: "We have a very solid district framework that encompasses our vision and a mission. Whatever you want to say about Warren, you know what we are about and what we are trying to accomplish."

A new cabinet member and a former middle school principal noted the district framework protects us from straying off the path we envisioned for ourselves and our staff, students, and parents: "Every person has a very specific role. If you stay true to the course with the understanding that when the data tells you to adjust, you adjust, and when the data tells you to slow down, you slow down, you begin to see positive results for kids."

Our constant review of our data in quantitative and qualitative terms allows teachers to adjust: "The openness to change obviously is critical, but at the end of the day it's a continuous improvement process that is forward-looking." The commitment to data to validate what we are doing and how we are doing it is critical and so meaningful for our teams at the district and classroom levels. As Tim Hanson, current superintendent, stated, "That's been a strength of ours as a district. We haven't been afraid of data."

We have placed our use of the plan, do, check, act process from the continuous improvement process that includes our goals and values with our interventions, and ultimately our assessment process, below.

Continuous Improvement Process

PLAN

Constant Data Review

Student test scores are used to identify instructional groups and to identify strong and weak curriculum areas and practices. Flexible grouping provides the necessary level of instructional support for mastery of standards. 1) Enhancing assessments 2) Increasing Data Access 3) Collecting new types of data 4) investing in staff learning

Instructional Timeline/Calendars

A timeline that encompasses all college-and career ready standards serve as a guide for instruction based on the need of the student group and the weight of the standard/objective/project. 1) Redesigning Curriculum, 2) Shifting to Common Core

ACT

Adjust Instruction/ Tutorials

Teacher teams (PLC's)/(Learning Log) and key stakeholders collaborate to reflect on assessment data for the purpose of adjusting instruction to personalize student learning. 1) Increase learning options for students 2) Deliver curriculum through digital age tools

Personalized Interventions and Enrichment STEAM activity

Provide intervention/time to re-teach non- mastered targeted College and Career Ready standards and STEAM opportunities for both mastery and non-mastery whenever possible.
*Adaptive software identified to provide a personalized intervention path.

DO

Instructional Focus Student and Teacher Facilitated

Using the timeline, instruction is delivered using multiple pathways, to address the unique learning interest, needs and pace of each student. Technology enhances personalize learning. 1) Increasing Personalization of Learning 2) Expanding Learning Time & Ensuring Relevance of Learning 3) Initiating Online Learning Options

CHECK

Assessment

District provides high quality assessments that are administered to identify intentional next step when mastery and non-mastery is attained. 1) Enhance assessment tools 2) Improving feedback for teachers, students, and parents

Intentional Maintenance

Based on individual student need, intentional and consistent maintenance of college and career ready standards through personalized digital content. 1) Enlisting parents as partners 2) Upgrading technology for digital age learning

Monitor

Continuously monitor and evaluate the process/progress of student achievement. 1) Examining responses to student behavior 2) Building strong connections with all students 3) Ensuring grant activities are successful 4) Analyzing data trends

Summary

To conclude, as superintendent, I took the board's goals and built an integrated instructional framework moving from Loop One, externally driven basic scripted instruction, to Loop Two, internally driven instruction based upon unique student needs and translated into three major outcomes: 1) college and career readiness at graduation; 2) a culturally relevant behavioral strategy driving classroom practice that created civility, order, and respect among students and between teachers and students K–12; and 3) personalizing learning for students and staff K–12. We used these outcomes to co-construct a framework with my district leadership team that united all the elements of past successful practices (descending Loop One) into a document to guide our decision-making over the next five years. We focused on the skills and dispositions our students will need in 2025 to succeed in an unprecedented era of change and uncertainty (ascending Loop Two). We adapted the Wallace Theory of Action into our student support system to connect and join our continuous improvement planning. This ensured our district's teacher and student support systems were aligned for student success and well-being.

The district framework has become the signature statement that has guided all decision-making. All staff can point to each element and see their place in the district's team thinking and in the implementation of the personalized learning strategy for themselves as well as for their students. In particular, the set of instructional support personnel moved from a prescriptive model of teacher support to the continuous development of teacher strengths and their voices in designing instructional improvement processes. That serves as evidence of the district's commitment to self-organization as the growth model for adult and student learning. These practices are aligned with Carol Sanford's (2017, 2018, 2020) specific set of organization practices, like self-reflection and self-regulation, that support developmental models of human capacity starting with internal locus of control, consideration of others, and personal agency.

We hope that you find my district team's experiences helpful as you pick and choose the events that transpired over the last ten-year period in public education in one urban school district of a modest size. We have included Anderson and Young's Table of District Effectiveness and offer it as a compilation of district factors you should consider as you rate your district effectiveness.

This book represents our commitment to the search for narratives of hope, resilience, connectedness, and fulfillment. We hope you find a lever or two to advance your own work as well as be moved to tell your own stories. Please share them with us at the Center for Appreciative Organizing in Education at aoeducation.net and we will publish them on the center's website to keep the conversation relevant and ongoing for all to learn from.

Lessons Learned

Personalized Learning for Staff and Students

- Any change required of students requires a change in teachers and the conditions of teaching.
- Personalization starts with individual acknowledgment of the need for change in a supportive and collaborative peer environment.
- As you consider an innovation, first think of how it builds upon what you are already doing and build it from there. If you are truly adding something new to teacher work, what can you take away from that work?
- How feedback is garnered and shared at all levels is crucial to successful improvement.
- Keep reminding everyone that implementation is a learning process, it is not a turn-key operation often or most of the time.

Reflection Questions

We believe the Warren success lies largely in its capacity as a board of education and a district leadership to frame its challenges in light of an overall purpose and set of core values that guided it through a ten-year period of storming seas or vertigo caused largely by external forces. Their district framework and their continuous improvement process built upon its instructional core process—the eight-step process—but early on Dena led her team to conclude that Loop One learning was insufficient to prepare students for their collective future. This exercise is about finding your positive core as a district and learning how to build on the strengths of your district's people, previous practices, and successes. Start there!

1. How might this chapter inform you and your cabinet and/or school districts as you reflect on the challenges and choices before you today? What are the sources of those challenges? Are they internal or external? Can you cite and describe the antecedent conditions? What did you anticipate or what did you miss?

2. What were the historical challenges your district team had to face? To what extent did those challenges and your response cause you to defer action, reduce programming, and lose quality staff?

3. To what extent did your district leadership follow and align their decisions and actions with your district framework and goals? What elements of your district framework were compromised and why? To what extent were the challenges and adjustments hurtful and harmful to student learning and retention of quality staff? To what extent do you believe funding was the major culprit? To what extent was talent leaving the

district a major culprit?

4. How has your culture changed over time? Can you calibrate the depth and extent of the change?

5. What can you do to reverse the internal context first? What actions can you take to move your district forward?

References

1   David Giles, Michael Bell, Robert Halsey, Carolyn Palmer. Co-Constructing a Relational Approach to Educational Leadership and Management. Melbourne: Cengage, 2012.

2   Carol Sanford. *The Regenerative Business: Redesign Work, Cultivate Human Potential, Achieve Extraordinary Outcomes.* Boston: Nicholas Brealey Publishing, 2017.

3   *No More Feedback: Cultivate Consciousness at Work.* Edmonds, WA. InterOctave, 2018.

4   *The Regenerative Life: Transform Any Organization. Our Society, and Your Destiny.* Boston: Nicholas Brealey Publishing, 2020.

5   Bruce Barnett, personal communication, 2020.

6   Gallup. "The State of the Global Workplace," 2018.

7   Jim Clifton and Jim Harter. *It's the Manager: Moving from Boss to Coach.* Washington, DC: Gallup Press, 2019.

8   The Tarrant To & Through (T3) Partnership. "Economic and Workforce Impact," n.d, https://t3partnership.org/about/economic-workforce-impact.

9   Ken Robinson. "Bring on the Learning Revolution!" Filmed February 2010. TED video, 17:42. https://www.ted.com/talks/sir_ken_robinson_bring_on_the_learning_revolution. "How to Escape Education's Death Valley." Filmed April 2013. TED video, 18:59. https://www.ted.com/talks/sir_ken_robinson_how_to_escape_education_s_death_valley.

10 Emiliana Vegas and Rebecca Winthrop. Beyond Re-opening Schools: How Education Can Emerge Stronger Than Before COVID-19," the Brookings Institution. September 8, 2020, https://www.brookings.edu/research/beyond-re-

opening-schools-how-education-can-emerge-stronger-than-before-covid-19/.

[11] Paul Tough, How Children Succeed: Grit, Curiosity, and the Hidden Power of Character. New York: Houghton Mifflin, 2012.

[12] James P. Spillane, Megan Hopkins, and Tracy M. Sweet. "School District Educational Infrastructure and Change at Scale: Teacher Peer Interactions and Their Beliefs About Mathematics Instruction," American Educational Research Journal 55, no. 3 (June 2018): 532–62;

[13] The Wallace Foundation. Central Office Transformation Toolkit: Strengthening School District Central Offices in the Service of Improved Teaching and Learning, 2013, https:// www.wallacefoundation.org/knowledge-center/ Documents/ Central-Office-Transformation-Toolkit.pdf.;

[14] Erin Anderson and Michelle Diane Young. "If They Knew Then What We Know Now, Why Haven't Things Changed? An Examination of District Effectiveness Research," Frontiers in Education vol. 3, article 87 (October 2018);

[15] Leonard C. Burrello, Linda M. Beitz, and John L. Mann. A Positive Manifesto: How Appreciative Schools Can Transform Public Education. Ashford, CT: Elephant Rock Books, 2016.

[16] David L. Cooperrider and Diana Whitney, Appreciative Inquiry: A Positive Revolution in Change. San Francisco: Berrett-Koehler, 2005.

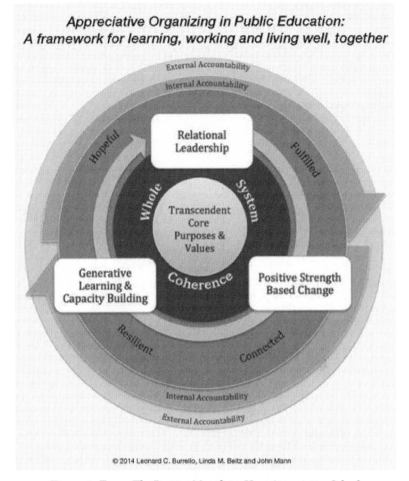

Figure 1. From *The Positive Manifesto: How Appreciative Schools Can Transform Public Education*

"An Examination of District Effectiveness Research," Frontiers in Education vol. 3, article 87 (October 2018)

District practices	Definition of effective districts (EDs)	Primary source of definition
DEVELOPING AND DELIVERING A HIGH QUALITY EDUCATION		
Have a district-wide focus on student achievement	EDs establish an instructional and curricular focus and develop a widely shared set of beliefs and a vision about student achievement, including goals for high expectations and closing achievement gaps. An EDs vision focuses on continuous improvement with a strategic plan for meeting goals.	Murphy and Hallinger, 1988; Leithwood, 2010
Invest in instructional leadership	EDs expect strong instructional leadership from the superintendent, district staff, and building leaders. EDs hold principals accountable for the quality of instruction in their schools, ensure principals are provided with support and professional learning opportunities that enhance their instructional leadership capacities as needed, and utilize expertise external to the district to foster system-wide instructional leadership.	Murphy and Hallinger, 1988; Leithwood, 2010
Implement professional development for leaders and teachers	EDs align professional development (PD) with district and school improvement initiatives and ensure that development opportunities reflect the needs of individual schools, administrators, and teachers. PD should be job-embedded, coherent, and district-wide EDs ensure that time and money is allocated to professional development.	Leithwood, 2010
Use proven approaches to curriculum and instruction	EDs establish student performance standards, develop or adopt a district wide curriculum and instructional approaches capable of achieving the standards, monitor the instructional and curriculum focus, and ensure the consistency and coordination of instructional activities. An ED aligns all elements of the technical core.	Murphy and Hallinger, 1988; Leithwood, 2010
STRUCTURING AND MANAGING THE ORGANIZATION AND ITS RESOURCES		
Facilitate alignment of the infrastructure	EDs seek to maximize alignment of organizational structures, financial allocations, and personnel policies and procedures. EDs seek to provide a well-conceived efficient system that balances loose and tight control allowing for autonomy.	Murphy and Hallinger, 1988; Leithwood, 2010
Interpret and initiate policy to align with change agenda	EDs analyze governmental change agendas to leverage them in the interest of district priorities. EDs ensure implementation of government initiatives, while strategically supplementing those initiatives to increase the district's impact. EDs also initiate policy that will support the district's goals.	Leithwood, 2010
Use evidence for planning, learning and accountability	EDs develop district information management systems, provide schools with relevant data, assist them in using it effectively, and create collaborative structures and opportunities for the interpretation of data.	Murphy and Hallinger, 1988; Leithwood, 2010
Approach school improvement in a directed and strategic manner	EDs are focused on improvement and design coherent approaches for school improvement that proceed in manageable stages and are integrated with existing policies and procedures. EDs build internal school and district capacities.	Murphy and Hallinger, 1988; Leithwood, 2010
Have an openness to and capacity for change	EDs continuously assess their successes and failures, have systems in place to monitor the impact of policy and program changes, are willing to develop new practices and processes, create structures and practices that can help to facilitate change, and mobilize continued support for reform.	Petersen, 1999, Duke, 2011
SUPPORTING AND LEADING PEOPLE IN SCHOOLS AND DISTRICTS		
Build and maintain good communication, relationships, and, district culture	EDs develop good relationships and a sense of community within the districts, establish collaborative and congenial working relations with school administrators and teachers, and nurture teacher-teacher relationships through support for professional learning communities. EDs also build external relationships by fostering board support and building close ties with external community groups.	Murphy and Hallinger, 1988; Leithwood, 2010
Foster district-wide sense of efficacy (4)	EDs provide extensive opportunities and organizational structures for teachers and administrators to develop expertise relevant to achieve the district's goals and enhance staffs' work and learning. School level staff should be held in high regard, have autonomy, and share leadership.	Murphy and Hallinger, 1988; Leithwood, 2010
Place importance on personnel and the roles they play	EDs recognize the importance of school and district personnel and the roles they play as "boundary spanners" between the district, schools and other entities. EDs carefully select individuals to work in key leadership positions, and develop their "human capital" to foster strong district-school relationships and communication and effective working relationships.	Honig, 2003; Honig, 2006; Spillane and Thompson, 1997; Honig, 2008
Focus district on equity	EDs have explicit goals focused on fostering equity, highlight inequitable practices and results, and establish and implement policies, structures, programs and practices intended to eradicate inequity, mitigate the negative effects of inequity, and support the success of all students. EDs align resource distribution, teaching practices, and personnel and staffing decisions with equity beliefs and goals.	Koshoreck, 2001; Rorrer and Skrla, 2005; Rorrer et al., 2008; Skrla et al., 2000

CHAPTER SIX

Teacher-Superintendent Relations: Retention and Development

Indiana's state tests have changed half a dozen times for students in the past decade, and with so much on the line, teachers, schools—and families—are trying to keep up... and limit a teacher' pay unfairly, and results in added stressors that can drive people away from the profession. —Jeanie Lindsay[1]

Teacher pay penalty dips but persists in 2019. Public school teachers earn 20% less weekly wages than non-teacher college graduates. —Sylvia Allegretto and Lawrence Mishel[2]

Over the past year more than 500,000 educators have rallied, walked out, or gone on strike in both red and blue states including Alabama, Arizona, California, Colorado, Oklahoma, and West Virginia. — Cindy Long[3]

The vertigo and what caused it: The status and conditions of teaching in public schools are undervalued and undercompensated. Teachers are expected to readjust and realign curriculum and instruction overnight with no time to learn. These conditions are leading to a severe teacher shortage crisis.

Further results from Sylvia Allegretto and Lawrence Mishel's the Economic Policy Institute report are summarized below to set the frame of the debate on teacher recruitment and retention into the profession.

- The teacher wage penalty has grown substantially since the mid-1990s. The regression-adjusted teaching wage penalty was 6 percent in 1996. In 2019, the penalty was 19.2 percent, reflecting a 2.8 percentage-point improvement compared with a penalty of 22.0 percent a year earlier.

- The teacher wage penalty declined in the wake of recent teacher strikes. The lessening of the teaching penalty from 22 percent in 2018 to 19.2 percent in 2019 may reflect pay raises enacted in the wake of widespread strikes and other actions by teachers in 2018 and 2019, particularly in some of the states where teacher pay lagged the most. Only time will tell if this single data point marks a turning point in teacher pay.

- The wage premium that female teachers experienced in the 1960s and 1970s has been replaced by a significant wage penalty. In 2019, female teachers were earning 13.2 percent less in weekly wages than their non-teaching counterparts were—a 27.9 percentage-point swing over the last six decades.

- The wage penalty for men in teaching is much larger than it is for women in the profession, and it too, has worsened considerably. The teacher wage penalty for men was 16.6 percent in 1979. In 2019, male teachers earned 30.2 percent less than similar male college graduates who chose a different profession. Only one in four teachers are men; women make up more than 76 percent of all teachers K–12.

- Penalties have worsened over time; some of the increase may be attributable to a trade-off school districts make between pay and benefits. In 2019, nonwage benefits made up a greater share of total compensation for teachers (29.3 percent) than for other professionals (21.4 percent). In 2004, nonwage benefits share of compensation was 20.7 percent for teachers and 18.7 percent for other professionals. These benefits, however we not enough to offset the growing wage penalty. The teacher total compensation penalty was 10.2 percent in 2019 (composed of a 19.2 percent wage penalty offset by a 9 percent benefits advantage). The bottom line is that the teacher total compensation penalty grew by 7.5 percentage points from 1993 to 2019.

- The teacher wage penalty exceeds 20 percent in twenty-one states and in the District of Columbia. Data range from 20 percent in Wyoming to 32.7 percent in Virginia. In twenty-one states and the District of Columbia teachers are paid less than eighty cents on the dollar earned by similar college-educated workers.

While volunteering at the District Community Center—an Indianapolis food bank—on a Friday afternoon, I was folding donated clothes in the back room when I saw one of the teachers from my district also volunteering there. She packed a box of food to take home for the weekend. As the superintendent of schools, I was heartbroken to know we were unable to provide her with a living wage. She, like many of the families in our district and in the country, needed community support to survive and feed her family. I came away from that day convinced that Warren had to find a way to pay teachers more. Not only do we have students and families living in poverty (the district has both middle- and upper-class families in the township), but the pay structure often determined by state funding levels barely afford our teachers an adequate salary. The status of teachers and their compensation was an annual anguish that I was not able to attack until my last year in office. We devote a whole chapter to increasing local funding primarily to support our teachers. For now, we want to describe our response to state legislation that impact teacher recruitment, development, evaluation, retention, and compensation. But it is important to place Warren's strategy on these issues within the Warren framework and within our commitment to being an innovative and caring enterprise that puts our teachers first.

Teacher Recruitment and Retention

The reasons for a declining pool of teachers lies partially in the constant churn of expectations and assessments that have become ingrained in many states over the years, including Indiana. The whipsaw of changing standards and the impact of those assessments on teacher compensation were part of the packages state legislators added to their reform efforts. Superintendent Tim Hanson observed: "Our postings three, four years ago would have a hundred plus applicants. Today we've had a few openings posted for a month and they're probably in the twenties or thirties."

Linda Darling-Hammond[4] added that a lack of input into professional decision-making, overly restrictive bureaucratic controls, and inadequate administrative support for teaching contribute to teacher dissatisfaction and attrition, particularly among the most highly qualified members of the teaching force. She wrote that only by professionalizing teaching will there be a new career structure in which improved preparation and professionally enforced standards of practice are combined with increased responsibility for instructional decision-making by competent teachers.

One of the issues keeping school leaders off-kilter and spinning is their ability to recruit and retain quality teachers. Vouchers, charters, and changes in funding formulas, rules, regulations, standards, and assessments have been designed in large part to undermine public confidence in our K–12 systems. The net effect of this serial attack has been to erode the foundation of the teaching profession from the classroom to the school district to universities that prepare teachers. Specifically, these damaging practices have disrupted teaching and learning tied to a set of compliance standards that perpetuates the state of vertigo that all educators find themselves in.

Teaching is a profession that seeks to ignite the imagination students need to pursue their own dreams. When it is not professionalized, younger generations will not see the value in pursing it. Education is not a business but a moral imperative to create a society that is open to diversity, order, and respect to individual differences. It is a career that deserves high regard; paying teachers a living wage is a moral obligation.

But teacher salaries are down by nearly 5 percent compared with before the Great Recession in 2007–08. It's not because teachers are younger or less educated, according to Michael Hansen,[6] director of the Brown Center on Education Policy at the Brookings Institution. In fact, the opposite is true: American teachers are getting paid less even though they are more qualified than ever. "Many people don't understand that it is becoming harder to stay a teacher because they are getting less and less money out of it," said Hansen. "They're actually more qualified than they ever have been in the past, and we're actually paying them lower." A 2004 Rand Corporation report[7] concluded that higher teacher salaries reduced attrition significantly, as did working conditions that embraced teacher voice and input into decision-making at the school level.

A McKinsey study[8] suggested that attracting the top one-third of students in America's colleges and universities to teaching would require school districts to greatly increase teacher compensation: "Raising the share of top-third+ new hires in high-need schools from 14% to 68% would mean paying new teachers around $65,000 with a maximum career compensation of $150,000 per year. At current student-teacher ratios, and applied to all current teachers as well, this would cost roughly $100-290 million for the large urban district and $630 million for the average state."[9] Another example of an alternative model of funding comes from Florida. Their governor proposed a minimum starting salary of $47,500 and allocated $500 million to do so, which was not nearly enough and actually created more problems of equity between young teachers and experienced teachers. The general public knows that teaching is a demanding profession, and they expect to be compensated fairly for that work, but the cost of retaining teachers is daunting.

During this COVID-19 crisis, parents are experiencing a double life working to support their families and coteaching their children remotely. Educators have become essential workers during this pandemic and have earned parental respect and recognition for their contribution to student learning. In our view, however, teachers have always been essential workers. The teaching profession has gained much respect due to the pandemic's stay-at-home mandates. According to a number of respondents in an AP poll conducted on April 30th, 2020, the pollsters found a new respect for teachers. The AP poll also suggested that 77% of the respondents felt that teachers should be paid more, and 69% felt that teaching is a more difficult profession than their own. Further, 55% of the respondents expressed that they would take more interest in their child's education post-pandemic. This data compares favorably with the 2014 Harris5 poll, saying that parents only respected teachers 49% of the time and students only 31% of the time.

In a 2018 Gallup poll[7] of K–12 US public school superintendents, teacher retention and recruitment was the number one concern for 61 percent of the respondents. Districts across the country reported teacher shortages, an issue not new and only growing worse. A 2017 *Washington Post* article found that "teacher education enrollment dropped from 691,000 to 451,000, a 35 percent reduction, between 2009 and 2014—and nearly 8 percent of the teaching workforce is leaving every year, the majority before retirement age."[4] The title of the article says it all: "Where Have All the Teachers Gone?"

"Where Have All the Teachers Gone?" Compensation at Urban Schools

According to the current Warren superintendent, Tim Hanson, a key element of the new teacher contract bargaining legislation changed. "No longer could you allow experience to move you up the ladder (increment). It could be part of the equation, but it could no longer be an automatic factor annually. This was part of the national anti-union trend to eliminate teacher tenure and an effort to further undermine public education, and re-allocate money to support promote privatization. The way our compensation model was set up enabled teachers to leave us and go to other districts and make significantly more money." For Warren, since the budget for teacher compensation was lower than in other more affluent neighboring districts, our rates were less competitive, making the salary differences between districts even greater. Elementary Assistant Superintendent, Ryan Russell added: "We had a lot of teachers leave for five, six, seven thousand dollars more a year. And it wasn't just the money. They perceived those jobs as easier jobs. They had less students of poverty."

The staff went on to observe that it takes a certain type of teacher to properly teach and connect with students in an urban school district: "Are Warren staff going to tell you that salary is important? They want to be compensated for what they do, but it's not the reason they stay in Warren. These jobs in urban America are more a calling, a vocation." Another growing problem is model legislation pursued in many states that allows "experts" in other fields to become teachers more easily through alternative certification pathways. This promotes the notion that "anyone can be a teacher." But one of the long-serving principals emphasized that working in an urban district can take a toll. "The job is becoming more and more difficult for our teachers. We are dealing with a lot of community issues that spill over, and trauma and anger that kids have." More than just compensation, there need to be pillars of encouragement for teachers. Upgrading teacher compensation and creating more professional working conditions are part of a structural solution, one that addresses the interrelated causes of the teacher supply and quality problems, rather than merely their symptoms. The principal argument continued: "I'm afraid if we don't do something to better support and retain our teachers, that we are going to have a revolving door. That's not going to be good for any school district or for our kids."

Impact on Students

The churn of teacher shortages and turnover inevitably results in teacher inexperience, under-preparation, and overall instability in classrooms, which greatly undermines student achievement. Schools suffer from diminished collegial relationships, a lack of institutional knowledge, and the expense of training new teachers who, oftentimes, will not stay. Research shows that stability, coupled with shared planning and collaboration, helps teachers to improve their effectiveness, and that teachers improve more rapidly in supportive and collegial working environments. High teacher turnover undermines these benefits, which are the product of shared knowledge and collaboration among colleagues.

Particularly, students in already struggling urban schools stand to suffer, though rural districts are not immune to the effects of a loss of talent either. Districts with vacant teaching positions have less-than-ideal options. They can use short- or long-term substitutes, raise class sizes, or leave non-classroom positions like reading specialists unfilled. These data are especially crucial when considering the work of researchers such as John Hattie,[9] who indicated the primary predictor of student performance is directly tied to teacher-related factors. A report by Rand Corporation[7] report prepared by Guarino et al notes: "Many factors contribute to a student's academic performance, including individual characteristics and family and neighborhood experiences. But research suggests that, among school-related factors, teachers matter most. When it comes to student performance on reading and math tests, a teacher is estimated to have two to three times the impact of any other school factor, including special services, facilities, and leadership."

Warren Township's Response

How did Warren Township deal with recruitment and retention during periods of high teacher turnover nationally? Teacher quality has long been a focus of the Warren leadership team, and the commitment to develop our teachers is a key component to success, according to both the cabinet and Warren's principals. Tens of thousands of teachers were hired in fall 2015 on emergency or temporary credentials across the nation to meet teaching needs, and the same pattern has emerged as schools opened in 2018 and 2019 in many districts. This problem will persist in 2021 as the pandemic recedes and schools fully open. When hiring individuals who are not prepared to teach, districts and schools facing shortages have a number of undesirable options: increase class sizes, canceled classes, use of short-term substitutes, or resorting to assigning teachers from other fields to fill vacancies. All of these stopgap solutions undermine the quality of education, especially for the students who most need effective schooling.

Our district staff felt our onboarding process was a significant factor in how Warren makes teachers successful as quickly as possible. We all remember our first year teaching because it is an experience one never forgets. In Warren, we begin by assigning teachers mentors, making sure they have multiple touch points with support. Superintendent Hanson explains it's as simple as sitting down with new teachers throughout the school year and saying: " 'Hey, it's been ninety days. How are you doing? What do you need?' Just allowing them that continuous improvement option. We're not expecting them to be perfect." Before, he explained, Warren was looking at the traditional criteria—the GPA, the undergraduate school, the nature of the pre-services experiences. "Now we are looking for mindsets—

risk-taking, more about the *why* you want to become a teacher versus what have you done to prepare yourself for becoming a teacher. Looking for that person who's going to connect with our kids. Relationships are the foundation and most important."

In 2008, Warren initiated an ongoing classroom-embedded professional development and technical assistance program provided by a team of eighteen instructional specialists. The instructional specialist work was designed solely for teacher development to increase the quality of academic instruction district-wide. The district's investment in teacher efficacy is the reason Warren's teachers were sought after by suburban districts looking for instructional specialists of their own and new assistant principals who understood instruction and how to use assessment data in a variety of traditional technology-based interventions. These skills built into Warren leaders help to inform the conditions of teaching to promote student learning to higher levels of proficiency. A neighboring superintendent shared with me that of three vacancies he had for assistant principals, he hired former Warren staff for all three of those positions because of their knowledge of instruction and how to support teacher development.

In Warren, we believe that personalization isn't just for students. The district's approach to teacher development as a personalized experience is equivalent to personalized student development. Professional development in Warren is individualized for each teacher, and team-oriented whenever possible. Our lead instructional specialist, Kate Schwartz, shared that coaching evolved to a more personalized approach when transitioning from a Loop One to Loop Two mindset (as in chapter 3): "It's no longer walking into a classroom and saying, 'We are going to work on this today and I'm going to model it and you are going to do it.' It's more on the lines of:

'What is it that you think about your classroom that you would like to do better?' " The emphasis on personalization allows for a greater diversity and fluidity of leadership, letting teachers adapt to a student's individual needs. Schwartz continues: "They have autonomy, and I think that is a common factor pulling them back."

What the new and existing teaching staff found helpful was the developmental application of civility, order, respect, and equity and excellence, the CORE framework: A social-character-building curriculum that offers clear direction toward the set of core values known to all staff and taught to all students K–12. CORE connects everyone to a professional standard that guides instruction and self-growth, and each person is expected to care for themselves and their own family (extended discussion of CORE can be found in chapter 4).

Another of Warren's principals noted that Warren consistently works to helps teachers and staff be successful along with its chief priority: student learning. He explained that Warren embraces high standards for all students, pushing them to higher levels within a rigorous curriculum. Warren encourages teachers to build data-informed formative assessments and use them to guide instruction and inform the multiple systems of support across subgroups of students. The concept of a Student Success period was championed by Warren teachers. Starting every day, all students had the opportunity to meet with teachers and staff who supported reteaching, provided additional practice and maintenance or remediation, as well as deeper learning experiences for accomplished learners depending on the needs of the student. Today, the district relies on integrated digital content and daily assessment data of student individual work as a means of measuring progress and when necessary, requiring more personal attention from their teachers and support staff. Encouraging high standards for our students cultivates a healthier, collaborative, and invigorating work environment for our teachers.

Teacher Evaluation in Warren

New state reform required every district to develop a teacher evaluation model that included increased observations, goals, and student performance measures; either that or select the state model RISE. With a former human resources director who was also a former peer principal with me, I looked across different district models for teacher evaluation plans. We knew the state would accept a plan that met their requirements, but equally challenging at this time was the need to close two schools due to the $3.5 million state funding reduction in our local district budget. The state required the removal of teacher salary increments, while we needed to rebalance the makeup of our district, and manage the need to redistribute and absorb 149 teachers through retirements, attrition, and the reorganization of a K–5 / 6–8 / 9–12 system into a K–4 / 5–8 / 9–12 grade level organizational structure. It is unusual for a state or a district to be given a choice in how they will evaluate teachers. In Indiana in the beginning, districts were allowed to develop their own evaluation system but required state-level approval.

Warren needed to understand the wide-ranging implications of the teacher bargaining law enacted as part of the standards and assessment changes and its impact on teacher recruitment and retention. The current human resources director noted that when the legislation changed, it affected what was bargainable and what was not: "The teacher bargaining law changed the calculus of relationships between teachers, administrators, and what counts as a part of teacher evaluation. A lot of the criteria that used to be bargainable was replaced by a guideline format only subject to discussion within district-teachers association deliberations." Bargaining parameters vary state to state. In Florida county systems can only bargain—"its wages, terms, and conditions," as in many right-to-work states.

Since the district staff always saw Warren as a cutting-edge district, we sought a new pathway to success: "We wrote whatever we needed to write to be a pilot district in that first year, 2011, after the new teacher evaluation law was passed." Our former human resources director worked with districts in the state for a year to observe how the others handled building a new evaluation system. What did she discover? "What I learned is that we were ahead of the game. We had a good working relationship with our teacher association/union. There was a lot of trust." Our HR team believed that the ongoing monthly meetings with the Warren Teachers Association (WEA) helped teachers feel supported and engaged in the implementation of the district's vision and new plan of operations.

Warren created a plan to keep close ties with the local teachers' association to make sure there was full transparency. Our HR director offered this insight into the Warren Plan:

> Principals are still learning how to gather evidence and better rate teachers. Teacher evaluation ideally is supposed to be about getting quality feedback and learning more about your practice as a teacher. Professional development is becoming more linked to what work you are doing with kids in your classroom. In a lot of ways, you are seeing things that are aligned so that everything fits together.

Our director of exceptional learners adds that the evaluation process has led to ratcheting up expectations for teaching students new content in new and distinct ways. While it may be more demanding for teachers, upping those expectations but asking teachers to teach differently has been better for the students. We continue to see growth happening and expectations shifting to respond to what our needs are now. From a principal's perspective, my team came to the conclusion that Warren has been very clear on that expectation to move to a personalized and blended learning model, but also knows we must give the tools to implement those initiatives. One said that we are a research-based district. Support is given, expectations are clear, and we give time to put it into practice and stick with it. He thought that the support and clear expectations that district level leadership provided through the Wallace framework led to our using the same language, having the same high expectations, and a data emphasis to determine what we are doing to help kids.

Superintendent-Teacher Relations

Meeting with the teacher's association and our HR director gave me a chance to remember what being a principal meant: listening and addressing teacher concerns about work conditions and the ability to teach without restraint. The district CORE social curriculum and a balanced calendar across the K–12 spectrum was a gift to teachers—a chance to reload and reenergize—during those two-week breaks, and an ability to work in real time with students who needed immediate remediation of the previously taught skills in a weeklong intersession.

But I believe what our teachers saw was my administrative team's ability to act when we were called to intervene in a difficult situation. We also regularly visited each school twice a year to hear teachers and the principal share their data and progress with my team. On these visits, we also discuss how we might further their academic and social-emotional needs throughout their school community.

One example of our ability to act comes to mind. During a monthly meeting with the union, it was brought to my attention that the third-grade pod, housing three classes, were over-reacting, unruly, and disrupting the school as a whole. The union was also concerned that students in third grade were being introduced to statewide assessment for the first time. This issue was further compounded by an unforeseen administrative transition and an influx of students from a charter school closure. Initially, I sent over my assistant superintendent who reported back that they needed additional support. We all went over to see for ourselves what was happening. During our visit, I told my team to go back to work and that I would stay the entire day at the school. Once I made that decision, I walked back to the principal's office and I asked who had a pair of flat shoes. She had a pair of Crocs, which I put on before returning to the pod. The students were quiet especially after I told them that if they continued to waste instructional time in their classes in the pod, they would be invited and expected to make up their academic time on Saturday with me. So they had a choice. This was not a new intervention, I have used this strategy before in my principal days.

After my day there, back at the central office, we agreed a leadership change was needed immediately and we could not wait, so we then took turns covering the building, from the assistant principals to the athletic director. It was all-hands-on-deck until we could make the needed changes. The response of teaching staff was one of appreciation and another layer of importance was that the third-grade test scores would be tied to their evaluation and, hence compensation.

The culture of our district was one that sees teachers as the most important asset. Teachers must believe their district and school leaders are competent in matters of curriculum and instruction, authentic in their interactions with them, ethical in all matters related to decisions and communications, empathic and considered of others, and professional in all relations with them, students, and parents. It is especially important that school-based leaders find and nurture the unique ability and human potential of each teacher. Our HR directors "always felt we had the resources to do the things we needed to do and leadership would support us." That level of support rippled through the district. The second HR director noted "that the Warren Framework offers our teachers a clear mission and vision that has set the tone for everything else we do. Dena's unique contribution has been to advocate that there is a need for new learning in new times."

Lessons Learned

Starting with the preparation and certification of teachers, I am recommending that universities prepare teachers in general knowledge and human development; learning and the content areas in their teaching; as well as the introduction of pedagogy including classroom management and positive behavioral support training and curriculum development strategies. But what is often missing in undergraduate preparation is a unit on the politics of education. We are arguing for its inclusion to assist future teachers in learning how to communicate with parents, deal with lack of support and funding, as well as accountability measures that are out the teachers' and oftentimes district's control and influence. Teachers need to understand who creates the structures, rules, and funding streams that impact them and their students.

It's our belief that the local school district must have an induction program and a novice teacher must complete a yearlong internship program under a master teacher in the local district. Recent research by Ronfeldt, Brockman, and Campbell (2018)[11] indicates that master or cooperating teachers mentoring pre-service into the profession impacts novice teachers' effectiveness. Certification is awarded based upon a successful yearlong residency as determined by the local district. Context matters in determining who is effective in differing circumstances, and that decision should be made by local officials. States retain approval of local district implementation plans according to preset criteria established by a statewide stakeholders groups of advisers.

Another area of interest is the need to increase the number of instructional specialists to support teacher development. Having these specialists connect digitally is vital. Kate

Schwartz, lead instructional specialist, described the value of such a device in this way:

> Because of social media we've really been able to increase the level of communication to something that is second to none. We've been able to highlight on a daily basis the great work that is happening in the buildings. Teachers have been able to form some social media friendships and relationships and find people they trust that are doing the same work. We always have people who are runners—people who really want to do the work and sometimes if they are completely alone they get burned out because they feel they are carrying the weight of the grade level, etc. Because of the different communications and having people who go across the district like myself and the leadership here they have been able to connect with people they wouldn't have otherwise known. And that's given a renewed sense of I can do this. I can do in my building what they are doing in their building and we'll keep going.

Recruiting and Retaining High-Quality Staff:

- Demonstrate your ongoing support of teachers by adhering those ideals and purposes through actions that impact teaching and learning.
- Keep reminding teachers they are part of a noble and most important profession and that that requires them to care for themselves too.
- Work to maintain a living wage for teachers.
- Teacher learn from one another in classrooms and in professional development teams.

- Teachers want individualized feedback and tailor-made support.
- The carrot-and-stick approach does not work, this is a transformative process, not a transactional one.

We recommend schools select their school-based instructional leadership based upon their teacher effectiveness and ability to coach their peers. I recommend a career ladder that begins with novice teachers in residence; advancing teachers in years one through five who are making progress; highly proficient teachers meeting district teaching and instructional standards; and in-school master teachers who have proven ability and success in moving students annually in a variety of conditions using a distinct set of indicators, but also selected on their ability to coach others; and finally, district instructional specialists who work in school as instructional master teachers in their efforts to develop novices and advance teachers into a highly proficient teaching staff school by school. Compensation should follow the level and breadth of expertise required to each level of development. Ongoing teacher development is the key investment of states and districts to preserve a teaching profession in danger of extinction.

Lastly, consider the seven dimensions of a teacher evaluation system proposed by Linda Darling-Hammond for your districts:

1. Teacher evaluation should be based on professional teaching standards and should be sophisticated enough to assess teaching quality across the continuum of development, from novice to expert teacher.

2. Evaluations should include multifaceted evidence of teacher practice, student learning, and professional contributions that are considered in an integrated fashion, in relation to one another and to the teaching context. Any assessments used to make judgments about students' progress should be appropriate for the specific curriculum and students the teacher teaches.

3. Evaluators should be knowledgeable about instruction and well trained in the evaluation system, including the process of how to give productive feedback and how to support ongoing learning for teachers. As often as possible, and always at critical decision-making junctures (e.g., tenure or renewal), the evaluation team should include experts in the specific teaching field.

4. Evaluation should be accompanied by useful feedback and connected to professional development opportunities that are relevant to teachers' goals and needs, including both formal learning opportunities and peer collaboration, observation, and coaching.

5. The evaluation system should value and encourage teacher collaboration, both in the standards and criteria that are used to assess teachers' work and in the way results are used to shape professional learning opportunities.

6. Expert teachers should be part of the assistance and review process for new teachers and for teachers needing extra assistance. They can provide the additional subject-specific expertise and person power needed to ensure that intensive and effective assistance is offered and that decisions about tenure and continuation are well grounded.

7. Panels of teachers and administrators should oversee the evaluation process to ensure it is thorough and of high quality, as well as fair and reliable. Such panels have been shown to facilitate more timely and well-grounded personnel decisions that avoid grievances and litigation. Teachers and school leaders should be involved in developing, implementing, and monitoring the system to ensure that it reflects good

teaching, that it operates effectively, that it is tied to useful learning opportunities for teachers, and that it produces valid results.

References

[1] Jeanie Lindsay. "Changing Evaluation Law Spurs Questions on Testing, Teacher Accountability," Indiana Public Broadcasting Stations, March 5, 2020, https://www.wfyi.org/news/articles/changing-evaluation-law-spurs-questions-on-testing-teacher-accountability.

[2] Sylvia Allegretto and Lawrence Mishel. "Teacher Pay Penalty Dips but Persists in 2019," September 17, 2020, Economic Policy Institute, https://www.epi.org/publication/teacher-pay-penalty-dips-but-persists-in-2019-public-school-teachers-earn-about-20-less-in-weekly-wages-than-nonteacher-college-graduates/.

[3] Cindy Long. "Average Teacher Salary Down 4.5% Over Past Decade," April 29, 2019, NEAToday, https://www.nea.org/advocating-for-change/new-from-nea/average-teacher-salary-down-45-over-past-decade.

[4] Linda Darling-Hammond. "One Piece of the Whole: Teacher Evaluation as Part of a Comprehensive System for Teaching and Learning," American Educator (Spring 2014), https://files.eric.ed.gov/fulltext/EJ1023870.pdf.

[5] Harris Interactive. "Perceived Respect for Teachers Has Declined," 2014.

[6] Michael Hansen. "Teachers Aren't Getting Younger, We're Just Paying Them Less," the Brookings Institution, September 5, 2018, https://www.brookings.edu/blog/

brown-center-chalkboard/2018/09/05/teachers-arent-get-ting-younger-were-just-paying-them-less/.

[7] Cassandra Guarino, Lucrecia Santibañez, Glenn Daley, Dominic Brewer. A Review of the Research Literature on Teacher Recruitment and Retention. Santa Monica, CA: Rand Corporation, 2004. https://www.rand.org/pubs/technical_reports/TR164.html.

[8] AP Poll, April 30, 2020 Parents have new found respect for teachers

[9] Harris Poll January, 2014

[10] McKinsey & Company. Closing the Teaching Talent Gap: Attracting and Retaining Top Third Graduates to Careers in Teaching, September, 2010.

[11] Gallop Poll, April 2018. Survey of K–12 School District Superintendents.

[12] Valerie Strauss. "Where Have All the Teachers Gone?" Washington Post, September 18, 2017.

[13] John Hattie. Visible Learning for Teachers: Maximizing Impact on Learning. New York: Routledge Press, 2012.

[14] Isaac M. Opper. "Teachers Matter: Understanding Teachers' Impact on Student Achievement," Rand Corporation, https://www.rand.org/education-and-labor/projects/measuring-teacher-effectiveness/teachers-matter.html.

[15] Matthew Ronfeldt, Stacey L. Brockman, and Shanyce L. Campbell. "Does Cooperating Teachers' Instructional Effectiveness Improve Pre-service Teachers' Future Performance?" Educational Researcher, June 2018.

[16] William Foster. Toward a Critical Practice of Leadership. In Critical Perspectives on Educational Leadership ed. John Smyth. London: Falmer Press, 1989

CHAPTER SEVEN

Superintendent-Board Relations and Transitioning Leadership

Dena recognizes competence and genuineness. That's how she deals with people. She knows how to spin our image in a professional way. She did not focus on how good the district looked on paper, but what made us real. She's not about the hype. — Mary Rehlander, Former HR Director

The vertigo statement and what caused it: School boards and superintendents across the nation have had to develop responses to state and federal mandates that have impacted local funding of education, teacher recruitment, promotion, salary, and retention of teachers and school leaders, student and teacher assessments, and other accountability measures that are not related to preparing students for post-school life in the twenty-first century.

It is always concerning to teachers when a new leader comes forth. They ask: What new initiatives will come in the first year or two under a new administration? How will these changes affect me as a teacher and my classroom of students? When the leader comes from inside the organization, people tend to expect the district to move in the established direction of the old leadership. This was especially true for me and the current team. In Warren, I was groomed for a couple of years by the former superintendent to lead the district. There was a buy-in from the board of education and for the most part, the entire school community. However, being the first black, female superintendent in the district's history and the second in Marion County in the same year, I expected challenges to my leadership and was sensitive to internal as well as external levels of acceptance and resistance. But I was open to new perspectives and new data and solicited both through my interactions with my team, teachers, board members, and those in the community.

Assuming the Position

The board wanted to continue to maintain stability within the district. They were aware of my history of success as a principal and as a district leader. From the beginning, I was always pushing the district to be innovative and to prepare our students for the future. I always pushed for an agenda that included what we should be thinking about next—not just the current Warren way and the state of affairs. The board knew of the previous superintendent's support of my work at the school and district level and encouraged me to obtain my doctoral degree, which I started some six years before I assumed the office of superintendent.

The board's charge, or agenda, for the new superintendent was negotiated through an external consultant, Ron Barnes, who I had studied under in my doctoral program at Indiana University. At the initial meeting with the board, the board's first goal spoke to the image of the district in the community: they wanted to increase the district's visibility in the community; they wanted an active and stronger social media presence to communicate with parents who could not attend school functions because of work schedules and other conflicts; and finally, they expected that I would support the continuation of the successful programs we had going in the district. The new federal grants did not come until the fall of our first year together, but the board had heard from me that we had to do better to prepare our students for the twenty-first century.

Too often schools and districts are portrayed in a negative light by the media. This underscores the annual Phi Delta Kappan poll results that find, parents like their own neighborhood school but not others. Districts should have a regular media plan and presence to promote and shine the light on the miracles that occur every day in the classroom. This was one of the things I was tasked with.

Fight for the Job

As is the case in most times of transition, there are almost always others within the school district who want the top position. Two stood out in Warren's case, both internal candidates. One was a longtime district administrator, former principal, and football coach, and the other was a district cabinet member brought in to serve as an early childhood director and later as our school improvement director. Both were highly favored by top leadership and each believed they deserved consideration for the top position based on either their loyalty and personal relationship to the former superintendent or in-district experience and relationships with the board of education. Both, however, lacked doctoral degrees and neither was pursuing one at the time, which my predecessor stipulated was a requirement for the position. One of the two had never been a school administrator and lacked K–12 instructional leadership experience. The other was the superintendent's gatekeeper and protector. Neither were outstanding practitioners of the Loop One instructional model being used in the district from 2002 through 2012.

When I assumed the position, both started to undermine me from day one, but I was undeterred. At the first cabinet meeting in July 2012, I put a sheet of paper in front of the full cabinet and told them if they did not want to work with me, they could put their names on paper and submit their resignations to me. Nobody signed the sheet of paper, but two people set their goal on making me a one-term superintendent.

What I did in response was wait and observe each of them. In time, each fell on their own sword and came to know that they were on the wrong seat on the Warren bus. Within a year, I moved the sergeant of arms from leading our secondary instruction program to operations over busing and facilities. He left after the second year to go to a neighboring district better suited to his mindset and skills. It took four years to move the second person, the director of school improvement, and for her to get the message that she lacked the trust and respect of her superintendent and her peers, and that her career lay elsewhere. She returned to her former position outside the district.

In the end, I would say that I was constrained only by the

sergeant of arms since he had a cache of support with selected board members and a long history with our senior high school team. But with minimal disruption, a discrete transition of the district leadership team took a total of four years to complete. Once those staff members were gone, they were replaced by two highly qualified leaders who I seamlessly incorporated into a cabinet of purpose-driven believers and doers committed to the framework and our vision. The district evolved into a collaborative and supportive team of leaders who supported me and one another and saw their mission as chief support to principals and teachers first and foremost in the pursuit of clearly articulated district goals for students and staff. As one cabinet member noted, "In cabinet, we could finish one another's sentences without fear of offending a colleague."

Typically, new superintendents have to wait out U-boat commanders already in the district. Others negotiate with the board and bring in new staff known to them, but unknown to the history, culture, and norms of the district; they all are on a steep learning curve. I adopted a "show me" strategy. Let me know what *you* intend to do to support our vision of transformation by your actions. I would not reinforce anyone who wasn't pulling us toward that vision and/or aligned with our strategy to get there.

Board Communication

The superintendent is the "Keeper of the Vision," and I shared my vision with the board and district team bi-monthly. I tried to live it each working day and night with all staff to keep the vision alive. One example was our Positive Social Behavioral System: At the entrance of every school, a design communicated the district's values and the priority we placed on CORE. Through visual representation—signs, window covers, banners—we shared the district and board's belief in civility, order, respect, and excellence and equity in plain view. This one element of the vision was embedded in the culture of every school. Our data on reduced behavioral referrals, suspensions, and expulsions in K–12 tell a positive story of the impact this intervention had on student behavior and the teachers' embrace of its implementation and effects.

Keeping board members in their lane and focused on the district's issues and challenges is hard work, particularly when an issue or a neighbor wants their attention. Individual board members' desires can supersede the district mission and vision, and my goal was to not let them derail the superintendent's and district's mission. How to do this is an important lesson for us all to learn, something not often taught in superintendent preparation courses. To keep the board engaged and attentive to the day-to-day flow of the district operations, I used Friday electronic review to update the board of past week's activity as part of the private board document file. If a board member was unable to access the information on their district computer, we scheduled a personalized technology training session with them and other interested board members to address computer access issues and how to gain access to board documents. Sometimes it really is just a training issue.

Every board member is different, and understanding their individual needs and aspirations is important to acknowledge appropriately and authentically. Generally, the board president is the lead champion or cheerleader supporting the superintendent's vision, helping communicate that vision along with other goals to the new board members and school community at large. Even with the weekly updates I provided to the entire board and holding individual meetings and phone calls with them, we still had board members say they didn't have necessary information. If an information gap persisted, I referred those individual members to their colleagues, the board president, or the board attorney. Sometimes they did not pay attention. Sometimes they were not interested in the topic. Sometimes they were simply comfortable with remaining uninformed. Sometimes board members are just too busy to process information, given their own lives. You must work with each member from where they are—they were elected by community members for a distinct reason.

My first year on the job, I wrote a midyear report based on the goals established with the board and the outside consultant but received little feedback. Honestly, I did not know what to think, but the federal grant did change the sustained agenda of the past. The president of the board was not concerned and expressed his pleasure with our team's work in spite of the minimal feedback. Thus, I produced a visual representation in notebook form with documentation on each indicator identified under the six goals within the superintendent evaluation protocol. Over the following five years I provided an annual report (See Appendix B) based on successes and challenges and the next year's focus centered each of our three foci: college-career readiness, PBIS, and personalized learning through a blended approach. I learned that engaging the board attorney is a good option when you don't receive quality feedback after submitting your annual report to each board member.

Board Turnover

In our state, board members are elected every two years. We had three members changing at each midyear election and four the next midyear election. During these fertile and uncertain times, it is the superintendent who has to balance the onboarding with the new board president. Arranging new member meetings with the Indiana School Board Association and walking them through the district's vision, mission, and established board goals and new policy discussions could be overwhelming. The board attorney is their attorney, not the superintendent's. This arrangement is locally determined.

While new board members may have specific personal issues, these issues are usually addressed during board work sessions, as the board establishes and reviews their yearly goals. I usually can demonstrate how their goals can and do fit into the overall district framework. If they have goals outside the framework, then the entire board, under the leadership of the board president, needs to weigh in on their significance during our work sessions, or we might employ an outside consultant to help manage the request.

It's not always easy to engage the board in new goals when they all might have a personal issue. However, I met board members where they were on an issue and tried to understand their perspective. While the board is updated weekly in the superintendent's report on a separate board doc, it is also important to separate the role the board president plays to ensure that every member is aware of the dialogue and/or requests individual board members make to the superintendent. Board members in our state could meet together but not if they were a quorum.

Changing the Board's Values

My approach to innovation and change was to connect the old with the new. I knew it was important to revise our goals when we planned to move to an ascending innovation Loop Two teaching and learning and how they would impact our vision as a district. At monthly board meetings, we showcased the district's data and extracurricular activities from band competitions to math bowl, robotics, and other academic performances at each school to personalize each school's path toward equity and excellence. The board meetings were the vehicle I used to validate individual school progress through the presentation of their growth, academic data, and deepening culture of civility, order, and respect with an eye toward achieving equity and excellence for all.

On the opening day of each year, I used that opportunity to both recognize our accomplishments and to lay out our vision and mission. Our rationale began with questioning Loop One, our past thinking. After years of teaching based on the state assessment and accountability benchmarks within a basic skill focus, my district team agreed that that was an inadequate path to the future. We knew the world was changing in real time and our schools had to be different. We needed to start to transform the mindset of our teaching staff to prepare students for the next generation of learning standards, which included embracing personalization through technology and the innovative practices that are emerging. We knew that the jobs our graduates would be asked to do were not the jobs of their parents. In 2012, we knew that the incoming kindergarteners, who would graduate in 2025, would be required to exhibit a new skill set, new ways of working and thinking critically, collaborating with others, problem-solving, and communicating. I started the conversation by making those class of 2025 students our North Star—our mission needed to align with providing students of the future with the necessary skills need to be successful and independent adults capable of supporting themselves initially and families they hoped to nurture and grow eventually.

The board in Warren was open to innovation. They were not afraid to listen to the ideas my team brought to them. It was a board member who suggested applying for the federal grant, which I jumped on, to her delight. Another board member brought policy ideas from her work with the Indiana State Parent Teacher Association and I found ways to incorporate her thinking with teachers and principals. Members were constantly aware of state policies that would affect the district positively or negatively. They were active in the state school board association and attended the school board national conference every year.

During this transition to Loop Two, a new board could be reconstituted with an election of either three or four new members. I used a series of communication strategies to onboard these new members, starting with individual one-on-one sessions with each new member as needed, weekly updates, board retreats, and work sessions, as well as using our monthly board meeting as an onboarding vehicle in of itself. Book studies were also a technique to bring new information and innovative thinking about the future. All of this was in addition to encouraging new members to take advantage of the state association and the opportunities to interact with external consultants and board attorney to help them understand their responsibilities, roles, and policy decisions. The board attorney was often asked to clarify board responsibility as distinct from the superintendent's responsibility, especially as it related to personnel termination or sanctions.

Diversity in Leadership

During this four-year period, I was concerned about diversity at the school leadership level and hired qualified teachers of color whenever possible. During those first four years, I searched for teacher leaders and assistant principals of color to promote internally to better reflect the composition of the students at each school. My team worked hard to bring over ten highly qualified persons of color into leadership positions in twenty schools and career centers during my year tenure as both deputy and superintendent in Warren.

I always kept everything professional and transparent. I held breakfast or dinner meetings with board members at state board or national events, but I never socialized with any one board member. Like any board decision that requires a quorum, my interactions were always group oriented and never individually oriented unless warranted. In times of tension and conflict within the board and between the board and superintendent, I would meet with the board president to uncover and clarify the tension or conflict at hand. My approach was to separate my personal or emotional reaction from the issue in order to clearly identify the underlying cause or source of the problem.

One example occurred in a November breakfast meeting, where I was reviewing the December board agenda with the board president and vice president. I was serving in my second term, had won the federal competition and brought $28.6 million into the district. We were about to launch our $40 million referendum over an eight-year period to support teacher salaries and renew a $140 million board-controlled project to upgrade our facilities. I needed all board members cooperating to make these community initiatives successful.

At this meeting, the vice president spoke up and said, "I guess people don't like you because of your race." I was shocked that he would invoke race as we were discussing the agenda. No one had ever said something like this to me in this context before. While I was in the role of superintendent, this board member's tenure was filled with tension around the issues of race and gender and sense of entitlement.

When he made that remark, I looked at the board president, feeling that this was an issue for him to address. Without waiting for a response, I quickly excused myself, paid the breakfast bill, went back to my office, and wrote a memo about what had just transpired. I called the board attorney and told him that I would not communicate with this board member again on the phone, by email or text, or in person even if he sat next to me at our monthly board meeting. I noted that the board president had witnessed the exchange and could corroborate what was said to me.

As I said in the opening to this book, you can only control your response to events, you cannot control the events themselves. When board members are having conflicts among themselves, with school personnel, or with the superintendent, the first recourse of the superintendent is to go to the board president and have them move on the solution within their governance process and with their board attorney. My choice was clear and the message I sent was clearer. That same board member caught up with me the following June as I chaired my last board meeting and apologized repeatedly. I told him I wished him and his family the very best and left the stage.

Summary

As superintendent, the role is 24-7. You are a parent, a counselor, a teacher, a supervisor, a comforter for parents in tragic situations, but most importantly, you are a listener who must engage with everyone. People want to be heard even if you cannot remedy the situation. You need to be able to read the tension or the joy and respond truthfully to who you are while realizing each situation requires a thoughtful and meaningful personal interaction. You are judged on your empathy and authenticity more than on being right.

The beauty of being a superintendent is the opportunity to share a vision and a mission for your district that is so clear and focused that you can taste it! It positions you to find and develop the district leadership team and promote talented teachers in their classrooms daily, to select principals who provide the conditions for teacher and students to come to school each day ready to learn and support one another, and the district initiatives that are coherent and provide meaningful work that teachers and students will engage in together. It takes teams of leaders at each level to build successful and fulfilling workplaces. When I toured classrooms in my last year, I saw the vision and our core values being embraced. I saw our students as self-directed, engaged learners. I knew I could leave the district and position. I felt that I had met my board's goals and my own personal goals and aspirations for the district, our staff, students, and community.

Lessons Learned

How does a district find, develop, and foster leadership development? Over a ten-year period, I found and encouraged more than twenty aspiring leaders. Certain skill sets emerged from my hiring history:

- They were student advocates
- They were great teachers and leaders in their schools
- Personally driven and vision driven
- Highly observant
- Able to give and receive feedback
- Demonstrated the ability to influence others to follow them
- Knew how to shut down the noise and keep the main focus, the main focus
- The ability to learn on the job and adapt into a collaborative leader style
- A work ethic and commitment to moving student success to higher levels

Here are additional lessons:

- The way you grow leadership in a district is to foster initiative and innovation on the part of everybody. The leadership modeling begins at the top, seeking and listening for ideas from everyone, acknowledging and respecting input with action where appropriate. The goal is to distribute both responsibility and authority as widely as possible to improve the system and its practices.
- Discover and articulate what constitutes quality leadership in your district. Make known the criteria that you are looking for in the leaders of your classrooms and schools.

- Look for leaders who can influence others to assume initiative and take responsibility for the whole organization.
- Expect every leader to have a personal development plan and one for each of those who report to them.
- Nurture good tries and reward them with your acknowledgment
- Know when to hold them and when to fold them—not every argument needs to be fought to its conclusion.
- Find mentors who can model and give positive feedback to aspiring leaders
- Give the credit away to others and accept the blame for mistakes as often as you can
- Create teams of talent that have demonstrated expertise and skills in their areas of responsibility and interest that meet a district priority. Give them the tools and support to do their work and observe who makes a difference.
- Encourage each specialized team to follow a similar district pattern of innovative development starting with a research base, search for exemplars to observe and visit with a full team of principals and teachers where ever possible.
- Come up with and compare against what others generated or others observed in practice elsewhere. Watch how they handle other team members and watch to see if they develop or learn from the talent of others.
- Superintendents are advised not to bargain directly, to use their attorney or HR director and/or a board member to directly bargain. Superintendents should reserve their approval to proposals or to the final agreements.

The questions around leadership development must start with how you challenge your staff and district leaders to get better. One colleague shared an idea that we observed in Warren: give them a task that is outside their comfort zone that needs really good study and thought.

Some final thoughts on superintendent-board Relations

- On-boarding new board candidates starts immediately. Superintendents have to use their board president, board attorney, external consultants, and the State Board Association to aid in preparing new board members to get up to speed quickly.
- Board's role is to set policy and hire only the superintendent who implements the policy.
- Have a keen sense to know when trouble is on the horizon.
- Hold annual board retreats to maintain focus and priority on board goals and district   communication to sustain informative dialogue and inform decision-making.
- While it is better to give more information than less, try to learn to balance it, and use different modes of communication.
- Lack of relationship and communications with the board is the primary reason for superintendent ongoing conflicts.
- Feed and water your board.

Reflection Questions

If you are a superintendent, or hope to be one in the future, here are some questions to ask yourself:

1. Identify your personal balance of leadership strengths and liabilities. What are your strong suits? What do you need to work on as a leader?

2. Develop leadership teams: Scale leadership in an organization by building relationships and leadership teams throughout the organization. What characteristics do you value in others? What of these characteristics best reflect what they can do to move your organization forward? For example: open mindsets, willingness to confront issues, transparency, follow-through, and the ability to influence others.

3. Build a leadership system: Profile high achievers and their leadership teams in a school district's leadership structure, and diagnose ineffective leadership and course-correct quickly.

4. Pick an enduring focus and stay with it. As one instructional specialist emphasized: "Don't allow yourself to become distracted by all the initiatives that come floating by. You will be successful if you say focused." What is one goal that you put first and foremost above all else?

What impressed us in our district was the ability of the district leadership to act. Within their purpose, mission statements, and core values, they had established a clear direction and a connectedness. The district consistently communicated its goals so clearly and could articulate action from one level to the next in light of the Wallace framework. I felt the culture was alive and well inside the classrooms of the district. We call this coherence. We have a few questions for you to consider around this elusive concept of coherence:

1. How do you determine if your district is connecting its parts into a coherent whole?

2. What is the narrative of your district? To what extent has it been communicated? Who believes it and sees it and can articulate it?

3. How do proposed changes in policy and practice fit the narrative? Align with the core values in pursuit of your purpose?

CHAPTER EIGHT

Innovation at the High School

A high school has always been a hub of activity situated in a complex ecosystem. Teachers demonstrated their commitment to student learning inside and outside the classroom from 5 a.m. to midnight. Robotics comes to mind. Moving a high school toward innovation has always been like turning a battleship around in a fleet of smaller and quicker ships—it takes a lot of time. —Dena Cushenberry, Superintendent

The vertigo and what caused it: Graduation pathways, structure of credits, subject matter content, and assessments hinder personalizing of learning, increasing the dropout rates. Policies often limited the learning progression and anytime, anywhere learning.

Transforming Warren's high school over the past ten years has been a complex and challenging move. With over 3,800 students grades nine through twelve, navigating that many teenage bodies through a school day and year is tough. When I came onto the district team and cabinet, the high school operated under the premise of "If it ain't broke, don't fix it." Football was a higher priority than anything else. The school leaders had great intentions but wanted to maintain the "old Warren way" with a baked-in status quo lens. The Warren way had worked for leaders who were graduates of the high school, so they thought, Why do we need to change?

But the demographics and context of the district had changed over the years. Community members remembered the nineties closures of many industrial businesses that could no longer support the employment of our graduating students. Employers today are looking for innovation from the next generation of graduates, with advanced skills in automation, technology, and Science, Technology, Engineering, and Math (STEM). Whether the high school staff liked it or not, change and the need for different skill sets had come. We needed to work on developing innovative mindsets in our high school leadership that would prepare students to learn how to collaborate and engage in their ever-changing and demanding futures. We needed to prepare them for a future that demands an openness to engage with unpredictability and continuous lifelong learning.

The Need for Change

In *The Global Achievement Gap* (2008), Tony Wagner[1] points out that our national graduation rate is lower than countries such as Denmark, Japan, Poland, and Italy. More recently, in 2019,[2] the United States doesn't even make the top ten list (which is comprised of Japan, South Korea, Georgia, Croatia,

Ukraine, the United Kingdom, Armenia, Kazakhstan, Slovakia, and Cyprus). The graduation rates vary from 93 percent at number ten to 99 percent at number one.

Our nation's graduation rate is approximately 88 percent, with the average state graduation rates in the 2017–18 academic year ranging from 74 percent to 94 percent, according to data reported by 17,404 ranked schools in the 2020 U.S. News Best High Schools rankings. April 22, 2020[3]

The six factors that impact graduation are

- Economic
- Demographic
- The ninth-grade factor
- Attendance and student engagement
- Course failure
- Internet and technological access

Only about a third of US high school students graduate ready for college today, and the rates are much lower for poor and minority students. Sixty-five percent of college professors report that what is taught in high school does not prepare students for college. The major reason? The tests students must take in high school for state-accountability purposes generally measures ninth-grade knowledge and skills. Primarily multiple-choice assessments, they rarely ask students to explain their reasoning or to apply knowledge to new situations—skills that are critical for success in college and future careers. Thus, neither teachers nor students receive useful feedback about college readiness.

A 2017 Hechinger study[4] found that "at least 209 schools placed more than half of incoming students in at least one remedial course." High school graduates aren't ready for college-level learning. The "Condition of College & Career Readiness 2018,"[5] prepared by ACT, tested 2018 US high school graduating classes relative to college and career readiness. The data in this report are based on more than 1.9 million graduates—55 percent of the students in the 2018 national graduating class—who took the ACT at some point between tenth and twelfth grade. The ACT was taken by the majority of 2018 graduates in twenty-eight states. In nineteen of those states, the ACT was taken by all or virtually all graduates, typically as part of a state-funded assessment program. There data indicated that:

- Slightly fewer ACT-tested graduates were ready for college coursework this year than last year. The percentage of students meeting at least three of the ACT college readiness benchmarks in the four core subject areas was 38 percent for the 2018 graduating class, down from 39 percent the previous year but the same as in 2016.

A higher percentage of students this year than in recent years fell to the bottom of the preparedness scale, showing little or no readiness for college coursework. A 2018 report[6] noted that a more realistic strategy for reducing college remediation is to weigh high school performance and grades higher than a standardized entrance exam. Many college counselors have argued that high school grade performance is the best predictor of college student success. But still the report noted that one in five students quit by the end of year one. Money is often a major reason for dropping out of school, but other factors do merit attention.

This discourse led to the birth of the Common Core standards debate, aimed at ensuring students are prepared for future jobs that don't yet exist.

Think Leadership First: Who Can Push High School Toward STEM and a Twenty-First-Century Curriculum

When I was appointed deputy superintendent a year before assuming the top job, the superintendent asked me to go to the high school and figure out how to bring it into compliance with our district model of teaching and learning as well as to move it from a chronic C rating in the state accountability matrix to a higher level. I learned that the high school's mastery of its own data was incomplete and flawed. In that one year we were able to assist the high school administration to evaluate how students moved in and out of the district, which impacted the school's graduation rate and the state score. Once we pointed out the discrepancies in the categorization and movement of students, the high school raised its state rating to a B. But we did not move teaching and learning forward. That led me to immediately start to consider how to find the leadership to move in that direction. By the beginning of the second year, I was able to convince the leadership solution I had found and put her in place.

The good news for the district was that the high school's career center, located on the same campus as the high school, had the leader we needed. When I approached the then director of the career center about two open positions in the district office, she told me she wanted to be the HR director so that she could use her counseling skills to the fullest. The other position was assistant superintendent for secondary instruction.

I knew we needed her expertise but especially the relationships she already had established with all levels of staff at the high school. She had the respect of the teachers, department chairs, and assistant principals, which gave her the social capital and influence with those responsible for educating the next generation of students. Her existing relationship with the adult education program made her an excellent resource and conduit that helped provide alternative pathways to graduation for students who failed or lost course credit due to poor attendance. Direct knowledge of scheduling was a key skill brought while navigating the many courses the high school offered almost four thousand students annually.

She persisted in wanting the HR position, so I recommended that she visit our HR director, who explained the position, its scope and responsibilities. She concluded her job description with, "I am the assistant principal of the entire district. Remember that there are seventeen hundred staff here and only seven hundred are teachers. I spent a great amount of my time dealing with the mental health and legal problems of our staff and families." When I called and ask which position my candidate wanted—the HR position or the instructional position—luckily, she declared, "I'll take door number two."

She went to work directly with the associate principal at the high school, whose primary responsibility was the school's master schedule and curriculum development. That associate principal was a curriculum leader in the district and agreed we needed to move the high school toward a twenty-first-century mindset. As a progressive innovator, the new secondary assistant superintendent was enterprising, finding apprenticeships with local business and promoting a dual credit program that led to associate degrees, and even supported a winning robotic team led by the new career center director and one of his teachers, who won state championships. Much of her work pushed toward modernization of the curriculum and creating opportunities for students to work at the career center focusing on vocational skills. During our negotiations for the new position, she started the first STEM career center in the state of Indiana during the lead up to her promotion.

The benefits of STEM are not only important in today's age of technology, but downright essential for many career pathways. According to Kelvin Droegemeier[6], director of the Office of Science and Technology Policy, "Students well equipped with STEM knowledge and skills not only provide a workforce prepared for meeting tomorrow's challenges to ensure our national security and economic strength, but also are able to function more effectively in our increasingly technologically sophisticated knowledge society irrespective of their chosen career."

In "The Progress Report on the Federal Implementation of the Stem Education Strategic Plan" published in 2019, Droegemeier discusses how despite the need for diverse STEM options in schools and better awareness of its value, many school systems have been slow to provide it. In the progress report, he introduces a five-year plan for implementing STEM education, "Where all Americans will have lifelong access to high-quality STEM education and the United States will be the global leader in STEM literacy, innovation, and employment." The three goals of the plan were to build a strong STEM foundation in students, increase diversity in STEM, and prepare STEM students to enter the workforce.

Keeping the high school up to date and current was a major goal of mine, and thanks to our new leader's efforts in establishing a STEM career center, students in Warren had the opportunity to look at a range of positions in the ever-changing and growing STEM fields. Thanks to her history of innovation and in-depth knowledge of the high school staff and curriculum, the high school started to move in the desired direction under her leadership almost immediately. While still laboring under a Loop One basic skills umbrella of thinking and learning, she was still able to help push Warren into the twenty-first century and beyond.

Diversifying Learning and Making Changes

In Warren, we do not believe in a one-size-fits-all approach to education. Through the federal grant, we significantly enhanced the education choices offered to the district students. However, to fully implement this grant, Warren required an instructional platform that recognized and honored students' differentiated learning interests and needs. We needed to provide multiple engaging and meaningful paths for demonstrating a mastery of high learning expectations aligned with the rigorous academic expectations of the Common Core State Standards and the New Indiana Standards. The vision for the high school was to embrace student-tailored options that would accelerate demonstrated learning in addition to required graduation coursework credit accumulations, all while simultaneously supporting students who struggle through the avenues they selected.

After a decade devoted to the development of the instruction process of continuous school improvement model, we made tremendous strides in student advancement and graduation rates in our high-poverty, high-needs district. In the 2011–12 school year, our graduation rate was 83.4 percent, and for my tenure the trajectory of the graduation rates increased each year to 87.9 percent, and as high as 90.1 percent in consecutive years. We increased the use of mediation in discipline practices to reduce suspension and expulsions. We went from sixty-nine expelled students in the first year to fifteen in the second year.

We knew our vision for the high school, of embracing student learning choices and student-centered support, would help our students realize their full potential. The needs of students, and not the structure of the traditional school day and school year model, would drive those choices. These were our goals:

- Students entering college would be ready for post-secondary learning—not facing remedial courses for freshman. Our students would enter higher education with multiple college-level credits attained through dual-credit coursework and pass rates on the College Board's advanced placement exams, as well as competitive SAT and ACT scores in their college applications. These opportunities would reduce the costs (and more realistically, the debt) of our high-needs students pursing college degrees. (Marcus[7])

- Students entering the workforce would be appropriately prepared and credentialed through state-of-the-art and rigorous career and technical education-training coursework. We would offer specialized classes, such as Bio-Med, Security Systems, 3D Technology, and Media Production, and state and national certification programs, meaning students could graduate with professional skills.

- We would enact student partnerships and extended-learning opportunities with Warren businesses and communities to add value to the prospective employer, allowing our students to quickly demonstrate workplace competencies and advance in their chosen careers.

With over twelve thousand students and a district-wide poverty rate of 71 percent in 2012 and over 76 percent in 2020, all students and educators would benefit from our pre-K–12 proposed initiatives. We wanted to transform learning expectations and achievement, measured by developing and promoting our online state and district capabilities and formative assessments aligned with the new Indiana Common Core standards. All students would have opportunities for extended day, week, or year-learning within technology-rich environs. We wanted to utilize exciting strategies featuring high-interest, student-directed alternative pathways that release high school students from traditional seat-time requirements, permitting them to accelerate learning or take more time. This mindset and programmatic shift was our commitment to Loop Two. We knew we needed to accelerate innovation in order to prepare our students for their uncertain and ambiguous futures of work and economic stability.

At the high school, if we expected more, we could achieve more through higher expectations for teaching through personalized learning. Personalized student support was enriched through extended day (until 7:00 p.m.), extended-week (Super-Saturdays), and extended year (intersessions and summer break) access to technology-rich environs and academic supports. High school students were provided with laptops, 4G cards, and Internet to ensure equitable technology and access for all learners. Through a computer-supported system for tracking students' strengths and needs, we introduced individualized goal setting and continuous monitoring of students' progress. This helped students reach academic and career goals, while also promoting student ownership and responsibility for learning.

We wanted to offer alternative pathways for in-and-out-of-the-classroom credit that closely resembled college and career experiences. These pathways encouraged post-graduation readiness and were tailored to students' interest and capabilities. Three examples of these alternative pathways are provided below:

- **Virtual Learning Opportunities**: High school students will have opportunities to work online, at their own pace, on their own time to receive competency-based grades that demonstrate mastery. These virtual opportunities will be used to obtain course credit for high school graduation. External partners will support the evaluation of existing online courses and influence district decisions to redevelop online courses meeting expectations defined in this proposal. Online content teachers will be identified and teacher schedules adjusted to support the needs of virtual learners. Professional development will be provided for content teachers and students and families of virtual learners.

- **Extended-Learning Opportunities**: High school students learn in part, or in whole, outside of the classroom in rigorous, relevant, and personalized learning business partner experiences, earning credit based on demonstrated course competencies. ELO educators will work collaboratively with highly effective teachers, community partners/business entities, and students (and parents) to: (a) Develop ELO plans, aligned to standards; (b) Provide the ELO business partner experience for students; (c) Students will make presentations of final exhibitions of learning (assessments); and (d) Course credit will be awarded to students who demonstrate mastered competencies, as evidenced during final exhibitions of learning.

- **Sports and Media Production Opportunities**: Students will train for successful television and broadcasting; manage a student-led profitable business, providing viable services to actual clients (and sustaining operational costs after the grant funding period). A bold concept in student training will offer an ESPN-like concept for the striving Indianapolis amateur sport market, and media video productions.

The specific outcomes and long-term objectives to our plan of action are detailed below in Table 1:

Alternative Pathways to Graduation (Grades 7–12)

Key Initiatives	Short-Term and Intermediate Outcomes	Long-Term
Virtual Learning Opportunities Students work online, at their own pace, on their own time to receive competency-based, demonstrate mastery, and obtain course credit for high school graduation.	**Short-Term** • **Quality Matters** evaluation of existing and traditional and credit recovery courses drives decision to redevelop or purchase coursework aligned to expectations • Partnership with ***ILearn Integrated Learning Institute*** established a staff review of relevant content and expectations to meet rigorous course requirements • Redevelop/purchase thirty-two online courses that met expectations • Identified and trained content teachers to support virtual learning of students and staff • Increased the number of students taking and passing online coursework	Increase student performance Provide greater opportunities for personalizing learning for grades 7–12

- Meet or exceed performance measures aligned with:

(a) Increased grades 7–8 ISTEP+ pass rates and high school end of course rates for English 10 and Algebra I;

(b) Reduce achievement gaps among student groups;

(c) Increase the percentages of Grades 7–12 students taking and passing online coursework

(d) Increase graduation rate from 83.4 to over 90 percent or more of all students

Intermediate

- Redevelop/purchase at least fifty online courses that meet expectations and expand the digital footprint in the high school curriculum
- Increase the percentages of students taking and passing online coursework
- Meet or exceed performance measures aligned with long-term outcomes

| Extend-ed-Learn-ing Oppor-tunities High school students learn in part, or in whole, out-side of the classroom in rigorous relevant and personalized learning business partner ex-periences, earning credit based on demon-strated course com-petencies. | **Short-Term** • ELO coordinator works collabora-tively with highly effective teachers, community partners / business enti-ties, and students (and parents) to: (a) Develop ELO plans, aligned to standards; (b) Provide the ELO business part-ner experiences for students; (c) Students will make presentations of final exhibitions of learning (assessments); (d) Course credit will be awarded to students who demonstrate mas-tered competencies, as evidenced during final exhibitions of learn-ing. • Meet or exceed performance measures to increased end of course rates for English 10 and Algebra I; Reduce achievement gaps among student groups; Increase the number of high school students participating in and award-ed course credit through extend-ed-learning opportunities; and In-creased graduation rates. **Intermediate** • Annually increase the number of content teachers participating • Annually increase the number of students participating and awarded credit • Meet or exceed performance mea-sures defined above | Increased post-sec-ondary readiness for college and careers |

Sports and Media Production Opportunities students train for successful television and **broadcasting;** manage a student-led profitable business, providing viable services to actual clients	<u>Short-Term</u> • Facility renovations completed and equipment installed • Course curriculum aligned to Indiana Common Core standards **Intermediate** • Annually increase the number of content teachers participating • Annually increase the number of students participating and awarded credit • Meet or exceed performance measures to (a) increased end of course rates for English 10 and Algebra I; (b) Reduce achievement gaps among student groups; (c) Increase the number of high school students participating in and awarded course credit through extended-learning opportunities; and (d) Increased graduation rates.

Behavioral interventions through PBIS	Short-Term	Increase
In partnerships with PBIS consultants and behavioral therapists, create a positive behavioral interventions support system for each school customized developmentally for all students with tiered behavioral interventions	• PBIS developed for all schools with a range of tiered behavior interventions • PBIS trainings in seventeen schools (pre-K–12) • *Parent University* workshop series (pilot in one elementary and one intermediate academy) to unite as a school community to promote positive social, academic, and emotional growth of our students • Decrease behavior referrals to principal's office • Decrease K–12 student suspension and expulsion rates • Meet or exceed performance measures to (a) increased end of course rates for English 10 and Algebra I; (b) Reduce achievement gaps among student groups; (c) Increase the number of high school students participating in and awarded course credit through extended-learning opportunities; and (d) Increased graduation rates. **Intermediate** • *Parent University* in twelve schools • Training for culturally responsive instructional practices in seventeen schools • Decrease K–12 student suspension and expulsion rates	student performance Provide greater opportunities for personalizing learning for grades 7–12 Increased post-secondary readiness for college and careers

As we continued implementation of blended learning through personalized learning, the look and feel of the classroom and how instruction was delivered changed. The role of the teacher and students begin to shift from a lecture model to a student-centered learning model, the CORE 4 (Integrated digital content, small group / targeted instruction, self-directed, instruction, and data-informed instruction). We continued to support both students and teachers through this transformation.

Our commitment to developing the social and emotional behavior of our students was a part of PBIS. Training our teachers and staff in how to meet the emotional needs of our students allowed students to learn how to deal with their feelings in a healthier manner, prompting less suspensions or expulsions, which had gravely affected academic success. Our school counselors supported the intentional teaching, practicing, and reinforcing of behavioral and academic expectations that led to the academic improvements we were making in our classrooms. Our CORE PBIS program was a paramount influence in the district's achievements in student academic performance, grades K–12.

Our consultants from Educational Elements took ongoing real-time snapshots our personalized learning progress, which provided useful reflections for our district leadership team. They observed in 2016–17 that: 1) individual school personalized learning teams (PLCs) were clearly leading the work in pilot schools; 2) The personalized learning "rollout" embodied the district's PL belief statement that "We all deserve personalized learning" students, teachers, and parents; 3) The district team was mindful in that they listened and responded to individual schools' needs with customized support; and 4) Communication and sharing implementations stories and successes occurred within and across the pilot cohorts and those cohorts that followed over the four years of the federal grant stimulus.

Future Considerations

Before we leave high school reform, we want to point out that we have been following the work of the Dallas County Promise,[8] led by Eric Ban. After four years, they have created a model blockchain technology that puts in the hands of students their entire school record, from eighth grade on, to enable students to control their own data and the ability to communicate what they have achieved beyond what is typically archived in a high school transcript. They call their process the Dallas County Life Cycle, published and operative in 2020, that allows students to make informed choice about workforce entry and college access at the community college or four-year institutions in Texas. Some fifty-two high schools and twenty-five thousand students are currently using this technology to control their own life history and future life choices. What is special about this blockchain technology is that it links all institutions in the community in a chain of communication that places the student at the center of building their careers through education. Next Generation Student Lifecyle Support created by the Dallas County Promise has the following objectives and has built a tool to enable students to control their life plan. The goals however need to be detailed below in Table 2 first.

Table 2
Double living wage attainment in a single generation

Workforce pipeline alignment	Career exploration and guidance	Connections to the workforce	Employer investment	Readiness, credential attainment, and placement
Define and align on region's highest priority living wage jobs and career pathways; regularly update and develop strategies to fill these jobs	Provide early and consistent career exposure and pathway guidance to inform student and parent choices	Support all students and young adults to gain the necessary work experiences, networks, and coaching to achieve job placement in their desired, living-wage careers	Increase the number of employers who are actively engaged in strengthening our local talent pool to enable economic prosperity for all	Grow and support the number and percentage of young adults earning credentials and job placement that lead to a living wage

Table 3
Next Generation Student Life Cycle Support

8th grade pathway selection	College Readiness	Work-Based Learning	CTE Certifications	College Credits
College enrollment includes the following elements: Financial Aid, Health Data, including vaccination records, Grad Exit Surveys, Transcripts, and College Enrollment and Tracking data	College persistence includes: college, dual enrollment, and seamless accelerated transfer pathways	W-B Learning	College Completion	Career Placement

Summary

In Warren, personalized learning refers to instruction that is now paced to the learning needs, tailored to learning preferences, and individualized to the specific interests of each student to the extent possible, namely at the high school. Learning is constant while time is the variable, enabling students to find an inspired purpose for learning because they are centered in their learning process, making themselves "the architects of the own learning." Through our one-to-one initiative, real-time data makes it possible to intervene when a student is struggling. We no longer have to wait until the student fails a quiz or test to discover that she or he did not understand the material. Furthermore, technology is proving to be highly beneficial in student-centered classrooms by helping us reengage at-risk students and retain students looking for alternatives to traditional classroom instruction.

High school successes are often slow in coming, but over my tenure, we moved our 2012 graduation rate from the low 80s to a 2014–15 and 2015–16 consecutive 90 percent graduation rate. CORE PBIS framework continues to support student-centered environments by teaching students character and behavioral expectations throughout all learning environments—cafeteria, hallway, restroom, but also learning/classroom expectations, such as independent digital, small group, and collaborative project work. Developing these foundational skills with our students allows theme to fully participate in academic instruction. In short, it is now possible to provide each of our students with the level of personalized instruction that enables them access to rigorous, standards-based digital content, meeting the needs of each student anytime, anywhere, and providing an alternative to the one-size-fits-all classrooms.

Other school successes are included below:

- Nano Line Team from the Walker Career Center placed first in engineering competition in state and second in engineering competition in Germany
- Grassy Creek Robotics Team placed second in state competition and sixteenth in world
- Pleasant Run Robotics received nationally recognized award
- The Department of Education announced the Walker Career Center as part of the first cohort of STEM-certified schools in the state
- Gold Brigade Marching Band earned first place in competition
- Warren wrestling team won state (2013–14)
- Football team won state (2012–13)
- Girls' track team won state
- Warren Township District received an Inspire and Engaged Award
- In my final year, 2017–18, the girls' and boys' basketball teams both won state—what a send-off!

Lessons Learned

Every classroom must address the CORE 4 via individual lesson plans and be observed when classroom visitations occur—through: 1) Targeted / small group instruction; 2) Integrated digital content; 3) Student self-reflection; and 4) Using real-time data to inform and personalize instruction. Within our district model of personalized learning, there are four non-negotiables:

1. Integrated digital content meets the course requirement and is teacher approved
2. Start personalized/blended learning with the freshman class and continue with each freshman class thereafter to ensure the complete transformation of the high school
3. The first three years of implementation at the high school focus on teacher development and learning how to implement the CORE 4. While moving through each freshman cohort, there will be no sanctioning teachers while transforming and adjusting their instruction during this initial implementation stage. Failure is an iterative process. The teacher evaluation and feedback protocols will be revised after this implementation period and after the third year—we reach agreement on a new set of metrics appropriate for this new model of instruction and on-going teacher development.
4. The district implementation liaison must have significant influence relationships from the principal's office, including assistants and department chairs to the teacher leaders in the high school. So selecting the right leader at the district has to come first.

Reflection Questions

It is common knowledge that turning a high school around is difficult and time-consuming. It touches upon disciplinary content, teacher certification, district policy, and state graduation requirements. So considering these factors, implementation science suggests you first must find and select the positive core leaders in the school's departments to lead the effort.

1. Can you select an implementation model to guide you? We suggest nirn.uncfgp.edu Research Center at the University of North Carolina to start your search.

2. Where do you start? How do you chunk your new content and process with accompanying expectations for initial to full installation of your model of practice?

3. How will you organize your leadership at the school, department, and teacher levels into interdisciplinary teams of influencers? These leaders need to be able to model, mentor, and process the implementation data from initial training to evaluation of the new practices that will become the basis of teacher performance.

4. What role will your academic counselors play in advising students to meet the state and district graduation requirements and how will they prepare students for career and college readiness?

5. What are the new metrics you and your high school team need to revise or add to as you seek to measure student outcomes? For example, might you consider seeking first semester college grades for graduated seniors who pursued college admission? Surveying employers of graduates to seek how well they made the transition from school to work?

References

[1] Tony Wagner. *Global Achievement Gap*. New York: Basic Books, 2008.

[2] Act Report on the Conditions of College Readiness, 2018.

[3] *U.S. News* Best High Schools rankings, April 22, 2020.

[4] Sarah Butrymowicz. "Most Colleges Enroll Many Students Who Aren't Prepared for Higher Education," *The Hechinger Report*, January 30, 2017.

[5] ACT Report on the Condition of College & Career Readiness, 2018.

[6] Kelvin Droegemeier, "Progress Report on the Federal Implementation of the STEM Education Strategic Plan," *Office of Science and Technology Policy*, October 2019.

[7] Jon Marcus. "More High School Grads Than Ever Are Going to College, but 1 in 5 Will Quit," *The Hechinger Report*, July 5, 2018.

[8] The Dallas County Life Cycle. The Dallas Promise. Summer, 2020.

CHAPTER NINE

A Dynamic School Community and Funding

We're here for the community, and I think some-times we as educators forget that. It takes a village. We have that theme here in making sure that the business, the health care, the not-for-profit, the ed-ucation and the religious leaders are all talking. We now have to figure out how not to lose that mo-mentum and that partnership and that conversa-tion. Right now I think we have the best collabora-tion, partnerships, conversations going that we ever have. But it's exhausting. So how do we keep that momentum going? —David Holt, Assistant Super-intendent of Finance and Operations

The vertigo and what caused it: State policy limits and controls the ability of local districts to tax themselves in terms of a one-day semi-annual count of students in attendance.

Separate state funds for capital projects, teacher compensation, and for students cannot be comingled.

At 2:00 a.m. on a May weekend, two young men were murdered, a third shot in the knee, and a fourth escaped unharmed in a neighboring suburb surrounding Indianapolis—all were Warren High School students. Throughout the weekend, I had conversations with our board of education, director of media, cabinet members, church organizations, and others to prepare for the impact of these young men's deaths on the student body. On Monday, I gathered the entire district team and took them to the high school to demonstrate our support for the high school students, administrators, teachers, staff, and the school community at large. While talking to the media and working with the county and city police about the perpetuators of the crime and their motives, we came to know the full impact of the loss. We added additional counselors for a full week to handle the tremendous stress and invited additional pastors and hospital staff to come in and counsel the students and teachers.

My presence was felt in hospital rooms and at funerals, consoling each of the families. I also spent time with community leaders helping manage their responses to the shooting. This is still an active investigation in our district and across the county for enforcement teams where the incident occurred. From this tragedy, one of our high school students rose up and initiated a new student gun violence organization called: "We Live" that attracted state and city political support after the horrific shooting in Parkland, Florida. This incident highlighted the need for our community to come together and offer support that extended beyond educational needs.

Warren: A Historical Perspective

The neighborhood that houses Warren High School was chosen in October 1994 as one of nine Neighborhood Preservation Initiatives (NPI) communities across the United States. The neighborhood became the focus of a Pew Charitable Trust initiative aimed at identifying neighborhoods that were strong and stable historically, but were increasingly showing signs of decay. At that time, the Far Eastside neighborhood reportedly was showing some of the same characteristics of urban decay and decline as the older portions of Marion County. Area residents and representatives came together in a series of meetings in 1994 to prepare the local submission to NPI, a plan and activity program aimed at improving the quality of life in the area. The plan was structured based on a needs assessment prepared by the Far Eastside Community Development Council. Areas of concern in the proposal addressed strengthening neighborhood associations, improving the identity of the area, improving recreational and educational opportunities for the area's youth, improving crime prevention, increasing area economic development, and providing more housing opportunities in the community.

Residential Capacity

The Far Eastside community consisted of residential neighborhoods that were plotted in the fifties, sixties, and seventies as a result of the postwar housing boom. A large number of apartments were built during the sixties and seventies. Many residents moved into the area to work at then-nearby factories and major employers such as Chrysler, RCA, Western Electric, and Ford, as well as a military installation, Fort Benjamin Harrison. The population grew by 7 percent from 1970 to 1980—from 28,686 to 31,688 people—compared to a 3 percent drop in Marion County during this same time period. However, between 1980 and 1990, while the Marion County population grew by 4 percent, the Far Eastside area only grew by 1 percent, or from 31,688 to 32,085 people. Housing units in the Far Eastside grew from 9,177 to 13,183 units between 1970 and 1980, but only to 13,961 units by 1990. In 2010, the population grew to 99,400 and by 2018 it grew slowly to 105,100 persons.

Chrysler, RCA, and Western Electric have since closed their doors, and Fort Harrison, a military training base, was in the process of changing its operations, leading to lower local employment opportunities. At the same time, an Indiana University study found that most Far Eastside employees worked in companies with fewer than fifty employees. The largest numbers of jobs were in the areas of services, retail, trade, and manufacturing. The study found that three-fourths of the workers living in the Far Eastside worked outside the neighborhood.

Currently, Warren Township schools are the second-largest employer of record in the area, with Community Hospital being the largest. That was not always the case. In the eighties and nineties, Warren was one of the wealthiest communities in Indianapolis. Eastside of Indianapolis is where some of the wealthiest people lived and wanted to educate their children. The nineties were the tipping point where technology changes led to many business consolidations and closures. Along with that came the beginning of school desegregation in Indianapolis, leading the nine districts surrounding the city to grow in student enrollment and to shift staff from their schools to the neighboring township schools.

These nine districts were most impacted by the desegrega-tion of Indianapolis's public school system. In Warren, there were many riots due to the changing demographics, which led to the flight of the wealthiest members of the communi-ty choosing to move to four districts north and northeast of Warren. In short, Warren is no longer a majority white school district. Fast forward to today, Warren is a majority-minor-ity community: African-American, 60 percent; Latino, 17 percent; Caucasian, 20 percent; and other, 1 percent. It has one of the highest murder rates for young men ages sixteen to twenty-four based on zip codes. Where you live is now often based on the likelihood of where you will die, and it's usually by gun violence. The hope for Warren Township was to form a community—we needed to find a way to give young people hope for a future they don't often see.

Community Development: Indianapolis East Side Redevelopment Committee (IERC)

In my first year as superintendent, the Community East Hospital's vice president of communications came to see me to review nursing services in the schools. Our prior super-intendent had worked with Community Hospital to identi-fy elementary schools in high need areas for health centers in their buildings for basic medical care and added nursing staff there.

His conversation with me led to additional meetings and gradually, the two of us sought out the mayor's liaison for the Eastside, and our local police department, along with a representative from Employ Indy, and the leaders from Finish Line, a shoe apparel company, and Raytheon Corporation, a military arms contractor. These companies and organizations were all asked to join the Eastside effort for revitalization and creating safe places for all community members.

The Marriott East Hotel leaders and managers hosted the meetings and served on the East Side Redevelopment Committee. The initial representative from Marriott East was highly sensitive to the deterioration of the neighborhood, suspect nightlife, and nocturnal adult entertainment activities. His concerns immediately led to adding an Indianapolis Metro Police Force member to the team's conversations about student and community safety. A five-part leadership team, composed of the Warren superintendent, the hospital administrators, the first and second major employers on the East side of Indy, along with the mayor's liaison, Marriott, and the Indy police department led a steering of ten that blossomed into over one hundred persons who became the Eastside Redevelopment Committee. Our expressed purpose was to develop a plan to address the social, health, and educational needs of the students and families and well-being of Far Eastside of Indy.

Some of the initial activities were a Finish Line grant that resulted in a playground at the Early Childhood Center. Second was a community jobs fair for graduating seniors not attending college immediately, which was held by Eastside employers who were recruiting for positions in the summer of 2013. An Eastside community clean-up day was organized by Warren Township schools, the mayor's office, Community East Hospital, and Eastside Marriott that brought together over five hundred students, parents, and community members to pick litter to beautify the community.

The Redevelopment Committee become a conduit that

reached out to the entire Warren community to increase the safe passage of students from schools to their homes. This committee became in 2017–18 the vehicle to promote the school community support for a local referendum to raise taxes for teacher compensation and retention, given the state cutbacks that did not return after the recession of 2008–10.

The committee and its members became the silent majority that assisted the district in passing both its referendum and the continuing need to maintain a bond structure for capital improvements. The committee continues to this day under new leadership in the district at the hospital and in the mayor's liaison office. This committee work was my primary outreach effort in response to the board's concerns addressing the image of the district, but more importantly, to improve the quality of life that impacted services to students, business, and community members' well-being. I cofacilitated the referendum work from 2016 through my tenure as superintendent in the district.

A Model to Consider

An April 2019 *New York Times* article, David Brooks's editorial "Winning the War on Poverty," which reflected on Canada's own struggles with impoverished communities, struck me as what we were trying to do in the Warren community. According to recently released data, between 2015 and 2017 Canada reduced its official poverty rate by at least 20 percent. Roughly 825,000 Canadians were lifted out of poverty in those years, giving the country today its lowest poverty rate in history.[1] Paul Born from the Tamarack Institute has written three books describing this process: *Creating Vibrant Com-*

munities (2008), *Community Conversations* (2012), and *Deepening Community* (2014).[2]

Brooks posited what poverty is like in America. He suggests everything is fragmented. There is usually a bevy of public and private programs doing their own thing. In one town there may be four food pantries, which don't really know one another well. The people working in these programs have their heads down, because it's exhausting enough just to do their own jobs. Brooks explains that in America, there is a "one donor, one funding program" where "different programs compete for funds."[1] This leads to a splintered approach to treating poverty: "the Americans who talk about community don't have a community of their own. Every day, they give away the power they could have if they did mutually reinforce working together to change whole systems."[1] In Canada, they took a different approach; they looked at community.

They "realized that a problem as complex as poverty can be addressed only through a multisector comprehensive approach."[1] They gathered people from a single community—"a quarter who live in poverty; the remaining group members were drawn from business, nonprofits, and government."[1] Researchers observed the community for a year, taking the time to understand poverty in that community and how it affects each group within it. After their survey, they came up with three goals: "How do we move people out of poverty? How do we eradicate poverty altogether? What does a vibrant community look like in which everybody's basic needs are met?"[1] They formulated a plan that focused on collaboration:

> A food pantry might turn itself into a job training center by allowing the people who are fed to do the actual work. The pantry might connect with a local

business that changes its hiring practices so that high
school degrees are not required. Businesses might
pledge to raise their minimum wage. The plans involved policy changes on the town and provincial
levels such as improved day care, redesigned transit
systems, and better workforce development systems.[1]

This experiment saw big changes. Canada's national government now had knowledge on how to strategically end poverty. The two most significant changes were these: "efforts in
cities to raise the minimum wage and expand the national
child benefit, which can net a family up to nearly $6,500 a
year per child. Canada now essentially has guaranteed income
for the young and the old."[1]

The most valuable lesson from this study is that working
together within a community is the best possible thing in fight-
ing institutional and generational poverty. The problem in
America is that our vision is fragmented; we only find solutions
to individual problems, not the gross issue. Paul Born, who is
head of the Tamarack Institute and worked on the study, believes "communities realize they can do more for themselves
if they work together across public, private and governmental agencies . . . [he] doesn't think you can do social change
without a methodology, without creating a community-wide
collective that impacts its structures."[1]

Applying Lessons in Warren

Characterizing this work in the Warren community, maintaining our district's engagement with our diverse community, was integral to the district community partnership. I was

uniquely positioned to lead in this role. I recognized that the religious community in Warren was an essential component of community life, with many churches present in our community. In addition, reaching out to the community leaders and jumpstarting the Eastside Redevelopment Committee were major reasons for our success while attempting to create community support structures.

I also knew that youth sports were essential to support students in the community, and a school district can play a major part in providing after-school services. Districts have the facilities and often the staff that can lead students and build out-of-school relationships with students and their families. Because Warren has both a stable yet transient student population with frequent housing changes, it's difficult to have consistent volunteers and stability within nonprofits. Not-for-profits are based on volunteers and selfless people who give tireless hours. As a community with high poverty, we do not necessarily have the option to call upon those volunteers. We recognized being in a community like ours meant you have to have alternatives available for families and the students.

With our school-based sports programming, which is a natural beneficiary of community youth sport development, we had the head football coach became the youth sports coordinator, his coaches and assistants ready and able to join in and help establish the stability our community needed. Having our highly successful varsity football coach, who was well known in the community, lead this effort added visibility and aided our recruitment efforts. We added the youth sport organization as his second and most important job on the staff after coaching football.

The Warren school district is now the community provider for football, basketball, baseball, soccer, and other youth

sports. Because that's important. You have to have those services for families to want to move in, especially if you are in a
high mobility community. You know there is always going to
be turnover, so you want people to say, "Hey, I want to live in
Warren." They're going to live in Warren because it's a good
place to live, they can find affordable housing, and the schools
are good. Right now, we've got all of those areas covered.

As I was closing out my career, I had been trying to work
with the city and parks department to increase green space.
In our community, green space and parks act as recreational
magnet for opportunities that families can access to provide
gathering space and physical activities for all to enjoy. We
simply didn't have enough positive and healthy activities for
families and kids. We looked at sponsoring events, bringing in
art and music festivals or other entertainment programs, and
working with businesses to give families the opportunity for
community involvement. We brought in the Harlem Globe-
trotters offset, the Harlem Wizards, to our high school. It was
less than ten dollars to get a ticket, providing a fun, engaging
event at a reasonable price for families. One of my main goals
was to find more of those cost-effective, community-engaging
activities, especially by partnering with performing arts organizations in our community. We wanted to bring events to the
east side of town, so families could have more opportunities to
interact with their kids. That was and continues to be important to me.

One of the IERC's strategies for economic development
is to provide job resources to graduating students immediately joining the workforce to combat violence. We also stressed
creating an economic environment that supported our current teachers. IERC coordinated efforts to make it financially
attractive for teachers who wanted to live in the community,

supporting them with fifteen-year loans to renovate their home or buy a home in the district. I also met with financial advisers who had insurance programs to eliminate or refinance student loans to match income, to help our teachers with their own loans.

Board and District Leadership

My board fully supported me as I fulfilled my contract goals with them, but even more importantly, I learned about what we still needed to do to support student life outside of the school day. We became, as noted earlier, the after-school option for many students who had no place to go. We offered structured academic options like robotics club and math bowl, or social activities like the boys and girls club and the YMCA. Our coordination with the Community Hospital also supported the district's health delivery system for everyday illnesses.

Top leadership in the school district must be visible and actively engage all sectors of the city and community life. As superintendent, your first order of business is to build a relationship with your board of education and secondly, build a distributive leadership model within your cabinet, with your principals, and with the teacher's associations based upon mutual trust and respect. Fortunately, for me, I was known in the city and community at large, and also by my internal leadership team. I could begin an active campaign to better the image of our school district and demonstrate a commitment to community well-being. I could become more entrenched as the school district chief liaison with the community.

Leadership participation in the redevelopment committee was crucial. Maintaining consistent monthly participation was a recurring challenge. Maintaining an agenda with real issues brought to the committee enhanced the relationship and connection between the players who could help solve the issue with a simple phone call. Trust and respect were built through these interactions. Again emphasizing the point of mutual commitment to community well-being, we prioritized this work on my annual calendar and encouraged my successor to do the same.

Let me close this chapter with our two most pressing funding issues that I wanted to wrap up before my retirement in 2018.

The $140 Million Bond Renewal

While all of this work within IERC was being done, we brought two issues of major interest and concern to the board of education. The first was to upgrade our facilities and make them future-ready and bursting with upgraded, integrated technology and infrastructure, which we could do on our own by renewing our bond authority structure with no increase in local property taxes. The second issue was paying and retaining high-quality teachers, increasing the security of each our nineteen school facilities, and the continuation of our innovative programs started under the Race to the Top funding. To answer the why question for a referendum, the board and I articulated several reasons in our rationale. They were "The Issues that Impact our Future." We chose five areas to portray our needs to the community in our communications. They are listed below.

Safety and Security

- Improvements to secure our facilities
- Ensuring that all vehicular access and circulation is designed with safety as the number-one priority
- Updates to video surveillance at all buildings

Facility Updates

- Drainage and infrastructure
- Improvements in building circulation
- Updates to classrooms and performing arts areas
- Improved learning environments

K–12 STEM improvements

- Modern classroom designs
- New and improved furniture in our classrooms
- Improvements in sound management for each building

Walker Career Center

- Updates to prepare our students for the twenty-first century
- Expanded and flexible instructional spaces
- Renovations throughout the center

Elementary Equalization

- Drainage and infrastructure improvements
- Expanded multipurpose areas
- Renovations throughout the schools to prepare for the challenges of tomorrow

We partnered with an Indianapolis consulting firm to help us plan and implement a public information program to communicate our aspirations and seek the community's support. The issues we stressed in the campaign were:

- Public School Funding (Tax Caps)
- Safety and Security of Students and Staff
- Improved Learning Experiences
- Recruiting and Retaining High-Quality Teachers and Staff
- Protecting Property Values and Taxpayer Investment

Since the district's capital debt was to be retired in the summer of the 2018–19 school year, the district team began to plan replacement financing for needed renovations as early as January 2017. Committed to being fiscally responsible and good stewards of the taxpayer dollar, Warren Township's board of education and administration agreed to first update our renovation needs assessment with an external consulting firm to study facilities, grounds, and technology. This helped to determine fiscal impact prior to the anticipated $140 million refinance of debt falling off in 2019 through a tax controlled project. After an assessment presentation from the consulting firm to the board of education, the board approved the refinancing controlled project and asked for community support, with a thirty-day comment period as required by state remonstrate rules. With no negative comments or backlash during the remonstrate period, the controlled tax rate remained in place and the $140 million bond issue passed with no opposition from the community. Thus, the continuation of structured tax funds allowed for building renovation and upgraded infrastructure, technology, and security cameras, as cited in the facility and infrastructure assessment report.

The $40 Million Local Referendum

In addition, in the fall of 2017, discussions began on a $40 million operating referendum different from the reinstated controlled tax project. Warren selected the consulting firm to develop a communication campaign for the May 2018 operating referendum. With continual systematic state funding cuts to K–12 education funds, we had to seek a referendum to provide additional security, school resources, and police officers, with the goal of improved school security. Our schools had increasingly fallen victim to outside forces manifested through the increased shootings. We found ourselves looking for ways to make our schools safer and more secure to limit external concerns and problems from outside the school campuses. Warren started working with a public relations firm to better understand our community's ability to support a referendum and the monetary threshold of the community.

The referendum would also allow us to continue our innovative programs initiated with the Race to the Top grant, as well as retain high-quality teachers. With that information, we decided to put a question on the May 2018 ballot asking for $5 million per year over an eight-year period for a total of $40 million. The purpose, again, would be to recruit, retain, and support high-quality teachers and staff; improve student learning experiences; make the schools safer; and to support and maintain innovative programs started with Race to the Top dollars that would benefit all of the students in Warren Township. The district team planned with our consultants Winston & Terrell for an entire year, but the final push occurred two months before the May 2018 vote. The cabinet and board members' presence was a significant factor. We were able to facilitate every community dialogue within each identified referent group representing community redevelopment—churches, civil organizations, nursing homes, and of course district-wide neighbor dialogue sessions, which any community members could attend. This effort was enhanced with the earlier rounds of work within the Eastside Redevelopment Committee. One effort built on the other. With 65 percent of the township turning out to vote in favor of the referendum, we felt the community supported our efforts for quality education and neighborhood programs for our students and families to enrich the collective well-being of all.

Lessons Learned

David Holt, our assistant superintendent of Finance and Operations, offered a perspective that became a mantra for me: "Together we can accomplish everything." We needed to demonstrate our commitment to the larger community by engaging with it directly in as many ways as possible. The board clearly told me that my goals needed to include creating a positive image of the school district in the community. They understood community trust and respect for our efforts were the key to obtaining and maintaining support for our future as well as our current goals.

As soon as VP of Communications Dan Hodgkins, from Community East Hospital, representing the largest employer on the Eastside of Indianapolis, reached out to me to discuss safety, mental health, and quality of life services in our schools and community, I quickly wanted to expand our two-person team into a full-fledged group representing government and other private or public entities. My goal was a complete team with an interest in how schools contribute to the well-being and safety of all of students, families, and our community members—a team with the resources and connections to better these students' lives. No one agency could accomplish our goals. We needed to align to support individual neighborhoods. We needed to advocate collectively to the mayor's office to ensure that the Eastside got its fair share of attention and resources, thanks to Hodgkins's liaison in the Redevelopment Committee.

As our work grew and deepened, we added members with different portfolios to include exciting connections throughout Eastside. The group naturally expanded to over seventy persons with the overlapping mission of increasing community well-being and quality of life of Warren Township residents. From safe streets, better-lit walkways, and patching potholes, to after-school youth activities, community policing, access to health care, and strengthening local employment and talent, to finally increasing funding for teacher salaries and retention.

Before I left the job, I worked to prepare my successor to understand that his role in the committee was his alone to represent the voice of the school district with his or her counterpart across the public, private, not-for-profit spectrum of agencies. Luckily, I saw the agenda of the Redevelopment Committee to be vigilant in continuing past efforts and redefining what emerged in federal and state initiatives, local employment growth, and migration of jobs—all of which might demand a local response.

Reflection Questions

If I were to participate in similar efforts again in the future, or advise my peers in the Warren community, I would insist on equal representation of local residents being a significant segment of the discourse prior to any action the group might pursue. So the questions become:

1. Who is missing from your dialogue?
2. Do you have sufficient representation of the actual clients who need and use your services and attention?
3. Have you spent sufficient energy listening to them share their stories and their history living and coping with the impact of past and current policy and practices designed to serve them?
4. What insights/data have your collected from your interactions with them?
5. How does their experience change or cause you to modify what you might consider in the future (resources)?
6. How are we not only co-constructors of the future, but how do we benefit from future innovative policy and practice?
7. What metrics do they suggest you consider as a measure of future impact?

Finally, let me suggest that as superintendent, you should think about this question: How does my board and staff participate in these community redevelopment efforts? In some ways, having a board member show up at events and meetings may be enough. We learned, for example, that our district staff was clearly the best communicator of our district needs, not the school-level staff.

So simply ask: Who needs to know about community redevelopment? And how do you invite their selective participants so as not to overwhelm any of your internal constituents?

References

1   David Brooks. "Winning the War on Poverty," *The New York Times*, April 4, 2019.

2   Paul Born. *Creating Vibrant Communities: How Individuals and Organizations from Diverse Sectors of Society Are Coming Together to Reduce Poverty in Canada*. Toronto: BPS Books, 2008.

CHAPTER TEN

Lessons for the Era of
Post-Pandemic Education

The vertigo and what caused it: Lack of infrastructure to support remote learning and threats to teacher health and well-being along with students and parent choice to participate were all factors that impacted the schools' ability to provide meaningful learning during the pandemic.

Fareed Zakaria, in his new book,[1] spotlights the broad lessons of the COVID-19 pandemic for the world. He gives us a framing device in terms what might come next while Microsoft and McKinsey[2] consultants offer their collaborative research on four thousand students and teachers across Canada, Singapore, the United Kingdom, and the U.S. as well as a literature search and interviews with seventy thoughts leaders from education, policy, and technology circles to highlight what this all means for education and educators.

First, it is important to remember the world's troubles are not just Made in the U.S.A., Zakaria rightly notes. They are rooted in ultramodernity: globalization, automation, alienation, mass migration, and the decay of the world's sprawling metropolises. This is the stuff of misery, he writes—and the fare of cultural critics since the dawn of the industrial age. Microsoft/McKinsey suggest automation could replace up to 50 percent of existing jobs in the U.S. alone and that lower educational level jobs will decline by up to 11.5 million in the nation by 2030. What will replace those jobs are workers with higher cognitive skills including problem-solving, critical thinking, creativity, digital skills, but most importantly, they emphasize throughout their research that 30 to 40 percent of jobs will require explicit social-emotional skills (4). They continued to argue that these skills sets, coupled with the urgency, speed, and complexity of change, will require students to come face to face with opportunities to innovate on a scale never before imagined.

Warren Township started its personalizing learning journey in 2012-2013. Its personalized learning model, optimized by integrating digital content and virtual technologies, played a critical role in shifting the paradigm from a standardized curricula and assessments. The student-centered paradigm is customized to individual needs with a greater emphasis on social-emotional skills. This focus on social-emotional skills in instruction and learning not only leads students to a richer professional career but will also lead to a happier and healthier personal well-being. This skill set is highly "correlated with a number of beneficial long term benefits including lower rates of obesity, substance abuse, and criminal activity and greater satisfaction in relationships and positive contributions to society" (12). Personal well-being is an essential element of early learning and should be encourage throughout society, not just in schooling.

Returning to the cultural context the nation finds itself in, Zakaria observes the deepening of the divide between urban and rural, elites and "deplorables." He notes the uses and abuses of cultural hegemony that have driven the forgotten into the arms of Donald Trump and triggered defections from the democratic left in Europe. The book's central message is: "This ugly pandemic has... opened up a path to a new world." But which one?

Zakaria believes many rich societies do not honor "a social contract that benefits everyone." So, the neoliberalism of decades past must yield to "radical reforms." Governments "will have to accept a more active role in the economy. They must see public services as investments.... Redistribution will again be on the agenda; the privileges of the... wealthy in question." Now might be the time for "basic income and wealth taxes" to ensure everyone can participate in a more fair and just society.

A critical reviewer writes: "Not bad for a supposedly capitalist mouthpiece. Yet this should not come as a surprise. Both *The Financial Times* and Zakaria's book urge a revolution is already upon us, and probably represent today's zeitgeist and reality. Free-market economics à la Ronald Reagan and Margaret Thatcher have had a nice run since the 1980s but he writes these days, COVID-19 accelerated and deepened the gulf between social classes engendered by the 2008 financial crisis. We are all social democrats now."

Zakaria notes, "Government in the West is back with industrial policy and trillions in cash. It is not a radical, but a consensual project. Taxation, a tool of redistribution, will rise along with border walls. For the more perfect welfare state can flourish only in a well-fenced world that breaks the influx of competing people and products." He goes on to argue we need quality government, not necessarily more government. It is our belief that we must find ways to connect more able-bodied citizens with meaningful work that provides a living wage. What combination of private, public, and government solutions can move us beyond only taxing the wealthy and subsidizing the poor? How to do it requires a political will to change the social order in America.

Lessons for Educators

Remember, preserving the status quo comes first—but a new paradigm is emerging—personalizing learning with a human capacity and living system mindset will appeal to most groups of advocates and winners in the old paradigm. What is clear to us is that education and health, for example, have never been really uncoupled from state and national politics. Two highly regulated institutions of society too important to leave in the hands of local politics either. From local school boards to state legislatures, community residents are fearful of changes that disrupt the status quo. Schools are inherently conservative institutions that strive to preserve what is and evolve slowly. As we have written earlier, the Common Core failed because it threatened to disrupt the hegemony of the educated and working classes. Social class and racial separation is enshrined and protected by zoning laws, banks and mortgages, and insurance companies all seeking to maintain the life hardworking parents and families have attained for their children. Tell us your zip code and we can often predict with confidence the educational achievement of the children and youth in that community. States have let the inner cities figure it out on their own, no more busing students of color or poverty to neighboring, successful, White suburbs, no longer subsidies for poverty, let the local funding support what it can and let us not use state dollars to create more equity between school districts. Finally, we cannot leave curriculum and textbook selection to local schools and their teachers, state legislatures need to control what students read and when they read it. But that is the old paradigm. That paradigm is broken and does not hold any promise in this post-pandemic world.

Personalizing learning through Sanford's human capacity paradigm. The nature of the student experience and therefore teaching in a more virtual world is more connected and accessible for each student to find his or her way through the Internet and its collaborative learning platforms, artificial intelligence, and immersive and mixed realities where physical and virtual worlds are blended, encouraging experiential learning. Personalized learning is now here and Sanford's human capacity dimensions that places the locus of control within each student and teacher rather than in external agents. It can enrich each student and teacher's personal agency to pursue their own goals and aspirations but it does require ongoing consideration of others in those pursuits. This is the new paradigm.

The most difficult component of the human capacity paradigm will be to promote and secure the consideration of others. What four years of the Trump administration and COVID-19 have exacerbated is survival of the fittest, individualism, and freedom from constraints like mask wearing to protect others from the virus. Moving forward we must commit to community well-being as well as recognizing the essence of each person's humanity, and freedom of choice, but to do no harm to self or others. The first implication of this proposal is the change in our individual and collective mindset but technically, is it the development of local and state infrastructure, that provides broadband and the access to the world of global knowledge and skill development.

Returning to the Microsoft/McKinsey research identifies three emerging technologies that are already providing significant tools to enable personalizing learning to thrive in our schools and communities. They are (1) collaborative platforms; (2) artificial intelligence (AI); and, (3) Mixed Reality. Collaborative platforms offered the means for students to interact with their teachers and peers in classrooms and remotely with one another to build their own learning communities and receive feedback. These technologies allow teachers to customize content, integrate digital subject matter into lesson plans that engage their peers in joint professional development, and to provide real-time feedback to students and their peers to modify instruction protocols. AI offers a means to assess student progress, create and monitor highly individualize portfolios of student work including lessons, homework, and practice opportunities, to get students to higher levels of mastery. Finally, mixed reality offers immersive learning that fosters social and emotional skills as well as their cognitive skill development. This option also creates opportunities to extend project-based learning and extended learning opportunities into the larger community with experts and mentors provide meaningful experiential learning.

Leadership Challenges. First and foremost, the leadership challenge is to make up for the lost learning that many students have experienced during the pandemic. But just as important, districts and schools have to reconnect and reestablish their relationships with students and families to determine the impact of the pandemic on them. If they lost a loved one or have others recovering from the virus. Districts and schools need to see if their staff resources like school nurses, coun-selors, social workers, and psychologists can be of any assis-tance to families coming out of the pandemic. A related issue is to come to understand why they did not participate in the remote learning schedule and to ensure access to broadband and working technological devices. The use of telephone apps as an interactive, connective device should also be evaluated as tools for learning and communication. Extended learning opportunities, Saturday school, mandatory summer schools, and other forms of in-person learning experiences need to be offered in an extended school day before the fall of 2021-2022.

Second, the toll on teachers and their ability to teach in-person and remotely simultaneously needs study and re-consideration. Teachers reported in the Microsoft/McKinsey study that all the potential benefits of a personalizing learning paradigm, teachers in all four countries surveyed, said a "lack of time, tools, and resources prevent many from doing more to improve their students' social-emotional skills and person-alized learning. Most lack access to technology solutions that already exist today that can help teachers better serve their students" (19).

Third, leadership challenge is the transformative nature of the switch in paradigms itself. Our Vermont friends taught in the late 1990s that the move to a learner-centered approach to student learning required first that teacher see students as individuals, teaching to each of them, not to the group norm. They taught us that learning is constant and is time variable. They taught us that students could and did set out their indi-vidual student learning plans with their parents annually, and could update them as needed. They taught us that students from first grade to eighth grade could and did build their ac-countability criteria for each project or lesson to judge their progress toward mastery. They taught that students could control their data and build reports that include peer feedback as well as feedback from their teachers. Curriculum revision also needs attention since it can limit the creativity and agency of students and teachers if there is not sufficient opportunities for them to explore their own interests and pursue their sense of purpose.

Curriculum is a powerful vehicle for enhancing student performance and well-being, increasing equity, and preparing students to thrive in and shape the future. And, now more than ever, to rediscover what it means to preserve and renew democratic institutions that have been under siege during the pandemic and the rise of populism around the globe. More and more we have come to learn and use the skills of investigative journalism—skepticism, critical thinking, and problematization should be at the center of learning and instruction in order to ensure students understand and can build arguments based on facts and evidence. The need to reemphasize civic participation as a member of a democracy and our responsibility to repair it, and delivery on the promises inherent in the Declaration of Independence.

The pandemic that has gripped the globe and the U.S. in particular is pushing school leaders and teachers to establish on the fly the transfer of learning from the classroom to home, from teachers to parents and grandparents, from the whiteboard to the computer screen. School districts are having to manage a huge shift in the provision of educational services. Of particular concern is how does a district serves students with disabilities whose educational plans require multiple services. What we are witnessing is a district like Los Angles, which is partnering with their public TV stations to broadcast educational programming to homebound students. Other partnerships with cable carriers are extending their bandwidth access to allow Internet services. Finally, Sal Khan recommends two thirty-minute reading sessions and math problem-solving exercises to prevent learning atrophy. The lesson learned is that planning for anytime, anywhere learning require infrastructure investment in digital learning and enhanced digital content. Warren fortunately had the federal resources to build out our capability.

To further this point, in an article published in the *New York Times* this past Thanksgiving (2020), David Brooks[4] wrote about a Jonathan Rauch[5] *National Affairs* paper entitled "The Constitution of Knowledge." Rauch argues that "every society has an epistemic regime, a marketplace of ideas where people hammer out what is real." All the stakeholders who create and share information from generation to generation "disagree a lot but they agree on a shared system of rules for weighing evidence and the building of knowledge." The knowledge-building process acts like a funnel in Rauch's view, sorting and selecting a limited amount of output that "survives the collective scrutiny" of all of the stakeholders in the community of scholars and practitioners who test and apply that research and knowledge. While we let "alt-truth talk" Rauch writes, "we don't let them write textbooks, receive tenure, bypass peer review, set the research agenda, dominate the front pages, give expert testimony, or dictate the flow of public dollars."

Sanford's (2018) book *No More Feedback* introduced the concept of developmental plans at the district, school, and individual teacher or principal or cabinet member. We have argued here that those plans could and should start with students and watch how teachers build their plans for growth and development that lead to student growth. Principals and schools build theirs accordingly, and ultimately, the district builds theirs off the needs articulated at each level below.

Clearly the pandemic, the tension between health experts and governors, to close business enterprises and schools, to protect students and teachers, has put school board members and superintendents in the crosshairs of parents and community members. Before we all complain too much, we should recognize the speed by which school leaders made schools safe for students and staff as they adopted health experts' guidelines. We should also cheer and enjoy the new status of our teachers as essential workers during the pandemic because what working parents have learned—that if schools could open even part-time, they enabled working parents the relief and support they needed to do their work from home or in other essential business and services.

Still, we know that some 30 to 50 percent of parents and guardians are furious with mixed messages and frustrated with the economic downturn and its impact of the opening, closing, and reopening of schools as the nation has experienced the third wave of the virus today. We have not found an answer to this dilemma. We do, however, believe an ongoing conversation should not pit teachers' health as essential workers against the health of our students and family members. Finding a common ground is essential; "do no harm" has to be our mantra.

References

1   Fareed Zakaria. Ten Lessons for a Post-Pandemic World. New York: Norton, 2020.

2   Microsoft and McKinsey and Company. The Class of 2030 and Life Ready Learning: The Technology Imperative. A Summary Report. Organization for Economic Cooperation and Development, 1–27, 2020.

3   David Brooks. "The Rotting of the Republican Mind: When One Party Gets De-attached from Reality," New York Times, November 26, 2020.

4   Jonathan Rauch. "The Constitution of Knowledge," National Affairs 45 (Fall 2020)

5   Carol Sanford. No More Feedback: Cultivate Consciousness at Work. Edmonds, WA. InterOctave, 2018.

CHAPTER ELEVEN

Concluding Thoughts on the Future of Public Education

The vertigo and what caused it: The pandemic has shined a spotlight on structural and systemic inequities in K–12 education and on the urgent need to provide strong professional support to teachers to teach not only in new ways but also to provide social and emotional support to students and parents in times of severe instability.

Looking Back

Redistricting in the district that led to the closing of two valued community schools while increasing the equity of access to quality instruction across the district. This move created a more intentional instructional focus on all students. As associate superintendent, I was charged with bringing the high school instructional program into line with our district's values and helped analyze their data. As superintendent we pursued federal grant money to move our very scripted curriculum to a more critical thinking, inquiry-based instructional model later supported by integrated digital content in a blended-personalized learning environment. We did it for our students, our teachers, our administrators—we really were able to transform education in a complex, standards-driven district. If you were to visit, our kids didn't seem or act like they were a group of students who were living in poverty (and of course some were not). They were enlightened, enriched, and proud of our school community.

Winning one of the sixteen awarded federal grants was a career-defining moment for me. The grant, which focused on college and career readiness, personalized/blended learning, and positive behavioral support systems, was essential in pushing the district toward equity—no exclusions. There were kids at the high school we "expelled," but we didn't stop their education. In spite of severely inappropriate behavior we gave them access to a personal computers and put them online with a teacher who would monitor and support them through their coursework. We understood that these students would one day be adults in the community and we wanted them to have a foundation for life. That technology provided an opportunity to keep students on track for graduation instead of casting them aside. We were proud to create a pathway for those students to continue school requirements outside the walls of the classroom.

The distruct team was proud to secure future infrastructure and stable funding sources with room to innovate for the next generation. Our debts were dropping off, so we renewed our $140 million local bond issue, which allowed for renovations of some older facilities that really needed attention, like the Career Center, which needed updates for robotics and engineering. Our community also passed the $40 million local referendum to hire and retain high-quality teachers. We focused our resources on safety: updating cameras and adding security precautions to the entrance of school buildings; and innovation: media production updates, expanded integrated digital content, and character education programs focused on civility, order, respect and excellence (CORE).

If I could go back, I would fight harder at the state level to demand a pause in transition from the multiple changes to state standards and assessments. I would ask the legislative leaders to help us understand why they were doing what they were doing. From 2010 to our current pandemic, there was a real movement by the state to destabilize and disrupt public education. We went from the federal and state requirements of No Child Left Behind / PL-221 to I-STEP Common Core—PARCC or Smarter Balanced assessment to Hoosier (Indiana) Standards to I-Learn to Pathways at the high school. If I were still leading the district, I would focus on importing the work of the Dallas County Promise and their partners at Greenlight and Salesforce to empower students to inform their post-secondary choices and to impact their high school preparation with more experiential learning experiences and increased use of mentors.

Most of the failing schools were in low socio-economic neighborhoods, some thriving outside of the letter grade given by the state. They claimed failing schools needed other options from outside sources to improve educational opportunities. But looking back, a lot of it was about creating and supporting private for-profit companies, with little regard to how these for-profit companies would impact public schools.

The emphasis on funneling public money through a voucher program of tax relief for families—up to $174,000 income—to attend private and religious schools will cause a major disruption to our public school systems. Encroaching charters drew hordes of students, then devastatingly closed, leaving kids to return to their public schools, overwhelming schools already in session for the year. This strained local resources for after-school programs and athletics—options that kids need. There are some good charter schools, and there are good private schools, but these private and charter schools are taking teachers from public schools. The teacher storage was started due to supply and demand. Too many options with little regard for who would fill all the new not-for-profit, charters, and private school teaching positions. And the devaluing of education has shattered enrollment at colleges and universities teacher education programs nationwide. Our students suffer with the churn of teachers.

Public Schools' Future

My concern is that the general public does not consider that education is more than a test score, more than an A or B or C school or district. Education is about preparing kids for life in an uncertain future and for jobs that do not exist now. Are the children in your communities ready to embrace the changes that are coming in AI, robotics, logistics? The public should know that public schools are the first option that can prepare students for learning how to navigate our complex world. Public schools never stop educating students in their neighborhoods—they are the "public good," and every child is welcome.

The constancy of state policy changes and the deluge of technology to hit schools and classroom has consumed district leadership and teacher discretionary efforts. It's gone from your basic keyboarding introduction to computer labs to constant access in the classroom and outside through cell phones and other devices and mediums and platforms. As educators, we must understand that technology and digital literacy is a necessity for navigating what life throws at our students and any job in a student's future. Students must have access to become tech-savvy—it's now their life, their future. Technology has been a game-changer for education if, and only if, teachers and children have access to innovate technology and its impact on how staff and students learn together.

Discovering what students need to be successful in their future is the North Star. Education should always be forward-thinking, looking toward innovative practices that improve the condition of teaching and learning. There's been a major shift from basic skills, which provided students with minimal education standards, to a more rigorous skillset that focused on depth of knowledge, design thinking. With rigorous and evidence-based standards, students can have the twenty-first-century education they deserve to be successful beyond school life. One-size-fits-all education is fast becoming an outdated practice. Students should not be sitting in a row listening to a talking head (sorry teachers) anymore; that's the old, industrial model of learning. In an anytime, anywhere learning environment, collaboration and access are key. We have to accommodate and demonstrate the appropriate modes needed to ensure students are getting relevant and fact-based, evidence-based information to show a level of competence. So what is it kids need to be successful later in life? That is what is left to discover as we enter another decade of education for the next generation of students in American.

I can't say I know what the future of education is, but I can say that we're in the middle of a transformation, one that we've never seen before, and probably will continue with AI thinking and platforms still under development. What another pandemic brings us in the next ten years is unknown as well. We have left the industrial based life of our parents to technology-enriched world where the unknown is the unknown. We have to start thinking, What is the future, and how can we bring everyone along? We can't just say because people are in poverty, they can't or they're this or they're that. We have to say, What are the things that our community needs to know? What's the technology they need to come to know? How do we get kids there? How do we embrace what we have and start systematically moving into the future and adjust along the way? What are our capacities to provide anytime, anywhere online learning at school and at home?

Lessons Learned as Superintendent: It's How You Respond

Let me be clear about what I think every leader must do first: They must wrap the most capable and passionate people around them as their leadership team. Choose people for different reasons and place them in jobs of high visibility and great responsibility. Finding or moving the right people to the right positions in the central office as well as principals and teacher specialists was one of my most important accomplishments during my six-year tenure and helped establish high-quality people for my successor—the district's personnel was filled with those committed to our framework and goals.

Leaders who designed and prepared newcomers for their old jobs and entered with passion and skills. It may take time to make adjustments for obvious political and historical reasons, but getting the right people on the right seats on the bus was crucial for me and should be for you. It's a sometimes painful but critical step for the message it sends about competence and commitment to organizational credibility and health.

A dramatic example of a commitment to put the right people on the bus came from an interview we did with Robert Avossa when he was the Fulton County, Georgia, superintendent. He saw many school principals who dress and look and talked like school administrators but he found that two thirds of them were unable to lead and challenge teaching and learning classrooms. He participated in the interviews of each replacement over a four-year period. He created a culture of excellence around people who could influence and impact the conditions of high-quality teaching and learning. More of us need to get our boards to support dramatic shifts of our talent; student and teacher learning are going to be the losers if we don't.

We wanted to see more districts co-construct their own district frameworks within their communities. Be intentional about how you communicate your purpose and core values. Be specific with your goals. Don't add something because it's popular, and don't take something away because someone said take it away. Do what you need to do based on your district data. Have a framework and speak to that all the time. When we looked at our district framework, we had our goals, but we were always talking about CORE. We were always talking about college and career readiness, personalization, digital content, and how to support student and teacher learning anytime and anywhere. Teacher professional development has to be contextualized and specific to each teacher. We provided multiple avenues for people to learn and to grow. It's not the same anymore. You can't give everyone the same thing at the same time. Everyone we know learns at a different pace that is why we subscribed to the Williston Schools belief system that time is variable but learning is constant and placing students in the position of being architects of their own learning is paramount. We shared the Dallas County Promise data platform that empowers students to portray their learning and accomplishments on their cell phones and can communication to anyone and any institutions who they are and have done with their education.

Superintendents need to know that it's not about the answers. There's not always a right answer; it's your response. There's a lot of tension right now in the world. We're trying to educate kids for jobs that do not exist, and even experts can't be sure what work is going to look like in the future. That's the struggle and the beauty. All of this feels like chaos, but hopefully, we'll have a better understanding of the future. We're in this really important time where we're trying to figure that out. We hope this text can provide your district with information, clarity, and guidance in these time of public education vertigo and this pandemic's impact on all of us.

Let us end with how we started, with another Jewish teaching from Jennifer Weiner She wrote, remembering Ruth Bader Ginsburg, that "you are not obligated to complete the work but neither are you free to desist from it."

EPILOGUE

You can't control what might impact or befall your district on a daily basis, but you can, as superintendent, control your response. And that is key. —Dena Cushenberry, Superintendent

The greatest change when moving from teacher, to principal, to superintendent was the increased scope and depth of responsibility. Everything that happened in the district would ultimately become my responsibility to respond and act on. First and foremost, I believed it was up to me to recruit, select, and develop a leadership team committed to our moral purpose and core values to promote and communicate the direction of the district, to find and deliver resources, and ultimately to support teachers in classrooms to ensure students' learning and community well-being. When you are the number one person, the buck stops with you. Your job is literally 24-7. If something happens with a student, a teacher, or an administrator, and it's two o'clock in the morning, it's your responsibility to get up, figure out the issue, and have a media statement the next morning for local television stations. The responsibility is enormous, and you have to try to compartmentalize, stay in the moment, slow the world down, and decide—and then continue with your life too.

Every single kid is important. We had to ensure that everybody—teachers, students, and staff members—were valued in every school and in the district office. I translated my knowledge on how to teach all children, and then engaged all staff in learning together to teach students to be critical thinkers with a much deeper depth of knowledge. I learned in the superintendent role that the leading edge of my leadership was to ask questions and learn from my staff at all levels and in all venues. I would ask essential questions: What does teaching all children mean for us? How do we teach kids skepticism, critical thinking, and problematization? How do we teach collaboration and the consideration of others while pursuing our individual goals? What is preparation for their future, rather than preparing them for our past? Oftentimes educators prepare students for our future, but we can no longer do that. We need to prepare them with a set of thinking and coping skills within a moral framework that emphasizes the common good. Personal agency, locus of control, and consideration for others are part and parcel of what is necessary for where they're going be and what they will inherit from us.

Right now, educators are in a process of change that we have never seen before. With the onset of technology, including social media platforms, and the onset of privatization and for-profit education and competition for state dollars, we don't know where we're going to settle. More than ever, education is about money: who can pay for education, our share of the public pot, who writes the books, and who writes the tests. But education is a public good and a social good. It is the one thing that helps all of us. If you don't have an education, you don't have a life.

In public schools, no student can be turned away. They can be turned away from a private school. They can be turned away from a public charter school. But public education is the one thing that people can depend on. No matter how rich you are or how poor you are, you can always depend on a public education. I wrote this book to say hang in there. Hold on to the narrative of schooling as the path to ensuring the common good and the well-being of all students. Reject the narrative of schooling as a means to grade and sort schools and students into A, B, C, D, and F tracks in order to increase the privatization of public education. This is just one example of innovation and transformation in an era of destabilization. There are many options, including innovative charter schools, that we can learn from together.

I believe it will get better.

ACKNOWLEDGMENTS

There are many people to thank for their help in the research and writing of this book. Without a doubt, my cabinet and staff in Warren Township—Dr. Tim Hanson, Ryan Russell, Mary Rehlander, Brian Simkins, Lou Schwenn, Pam Griffin, Allison Woods, and David Holt—as well as my administrative assistants, Carol Graham, Jane Glover, and Kim Asbury. A special callout to James Taylor for all of the counseling and after-school programs that allowed the continuation of the education of students facing suspension and expulsion. A special thank-you to all who participated in the Race to the Top grant as well.

My board deserves special mention for their continuous support over ten years as deputy superintendent and superintendent of schools, Julie French, Rachel Burke, Gloria Williams, Lynn Matchett, Terri Amos, and Howard Dorsey gave me the impetus to tell our story in this book. I want to thank David Randall for his encouragement and his support of my education and work, and my staff at Liberty Park Elementary School, where I learned to lead a beautifully diverse school, and eventually a diverse school district, supported by my principal colleagues, especially Phil Talbert, Susan Howard, and Steve Foster.

Thank you to my research colleague in the preparation of this manuscript, Robin Miles, who visited the district repeatedly and conducted twenty-five interviews with Warren District staff, including our instructional specialist cohort.

To the editors at Elephant Rock Books: Chris Morris for editing the initial draft, Sabrina Cofer and Anne McPeak for the final drafts, to Kristiana Torres for supervising the book's layout, and to their mentor, Jotham Burrello, publisher. Finally, I would like to extend my full-throated thanks to three reviewers of early complete drafts: Bruce Barnett from the University of Texas–San Antonio, professor of educational leadership studies; William Miller, the executive director of the Michigan Association of Intermediate School Administrators and former superintendent of Washtenaw Intermediate School District, Ann Arbor; and Ronald Barnes, clinical professor of educational leadership and policy studies at Indiana University. The final external reviewers included Alvin Taylor, former superintendent of Meridian, Mississippi, and a clinical professor at University of Montevallo in Alabama; Ruth Melton, the former Florida School Boards Association's policy guru; Doris Downing from Indianapolis, Indiana.

Finally, I want to dedicate this work to the teachers, students, and staff of Warren Township who made our edict to innovate, educate, and inspire come to life. Together, we created the conditions for meaningful anytime, anywhere learning.

Appendices

Appendix A

Wallace Framework

APPENDIX A: 21st Century Readiness Skills – Wallace Framework

(1) Student will model civility, order, respect, and excellence.		
Teachers will:	**Building Administrators will:**	**District Office Admin. will:**
• Model	• Share data with staff	• Provide data
• **Build relationships**	• Be consistent with plan and implementations	• Provide money
• Develop class plans (aligned to Building plans)	• Model for teachers and students	• **Communicate with all stakeholders on data and training**
• Build relationships	• Give school wide staff recognition	• Give technical support
• Teach CORE plans		• Provide training
• Analyze data for trends constantly	• **Support the plan**	• Recognize bldg administration
• Monitor reactions/ decisions	• Work with parents	• Revise R&R handbook
• Speak to students as if they believe they all belong here	• Lead communication	• Coordinate with PBIS
	• Provide PD	
	• Discipline data meetings as needed	

(2) Student will have access to their achievement and growth data and set goals based on data points to personalize their learning.		
Teachers will:	**Building Administrators will:**	**District Office Admin. will:**
• See that students can easily access their own personal data (incorporating a system of accountability with scheduled regularity) • **Stay current in recording student data** • Assist students in data interpretation and goal setting	• Monitor teachers data collection and reporting • **Collaborate with chairs and APs to include data collection as a professional expectation** • Provide school wide professional development	• **Create an efficient and comprehensive data warehouse** • Collaborate with principals to include data collection as a professional expectation • Provide district wide professional development
(3) Student will have choice and voice in their learning process in terms of content, pace, process, and product.		
Teachers will:	**Building Administrators will:**	**District Office Admin. will:**
• Be proficient in content level • **Be receptive to options and choice for students** • Organize and understand technology • "Coach" students vs. direct students • Know how to properly assess • Allow students to "create" products	• Seek new skill sets for instruction in hiring practices • Allow teachers to take risks • Agree that the daily schedule will look different • Trust the process • Look at teams - need technologically savy person for support • **Shift PD and time for collaboration**	• Recognize calendar parameters may need reassessment • Redesign classroom setup • Provide examples of clear vision • **Monitor and train** • Allow for risk taking • Embrace new ways to look at teachers in their classrooms

(4) Student will learn and demonstrate competency (mastery) with the content and skills of college and career standards.		
Teachers will:	**Building Administrators will:**	**District Office Admin. will:**
• **Deliver effective instruction** • Participate in PD • Use data driven instruction • Have an understanding of district vision • Personalize student instruction • Communicate student progress data with parents	• **Understand and support district plan and timeline** • Understand district vision • Coach and support instruction • Ensure certainty	• Provide PD • Set clear expectations that are realistic • Create a timeline • Communicate with community members • **Ensure certainty**

(5) Students learning will be characterized by regular opportunities for project-based learning anchored in mastery of college and career ready standards.		
Teachers will:	**Building Administrators will:**	**District Office Admin. will:**
☐ Serve and provide excellence as a facilitator ☐ **Seek out community partnerships** ☐ Participate in professional development ☐ Have a good understanding of the standards and objective of PBL ☐ Establish protocols for the class ☐ Integrate and model CORE in all aspects of PBL	☐ **Coordinate and participate in professional development** ☐ Provide financial support through budgeting ☐ Be mindful of PBL while developing the master schedule	☐ Set expectations that PBL will occur ☐ Coordinate and participate in professional development ☐ Provide financial support for PBL ☐ **Set a framework for what PBL will look like**

(6) Student will demonstrate competency with information age skills such as collaboration, critical thinking, and problem solving (beyond the walls of the classrooms).		
Teachers will:	**Building Administrators will:**	**District Office Admin. will:**
• Use a web-based system to house curriculum • **Flip classes** • Allow collaboration between students in/out of class • Participate in PD	• **Provide PD for teachers and staff** • Monitor implementation and provide constructive feedback • Model flipped staff meetings	• **Cast the vision for learning beyond the walls of the classroom** • Provide tools for staff and students • Provide professional development • Model flipped classroom PD

(7) Student will read and write on or above grade level across content.		
Teachers will:	**Building Administrators will:**	**District Office Admin. will:**
• Assure that reading and writing instruction will occur across disciplines	• Provide time for collaboration and planning for high quality instruction	• **Provide and set a vision and direction that is measurable and goal oriented with benchmarks**
• Receive PD that makes cross disciplinary literacy instruction possible	• Analyze trends	• Celebrate progress
• Access and assess data on student reading/writing skills regularly	• Provide resources and interventions in support of student needs	• Allocate funds aligned to this priority
• Use technology to personalize reading and writing instruction	• Expect focused time instructionally for students with greatest needs	• Identify best practices
• **Collaborate with each other and library media colleagues on ideas, strategies, and resources to support this goal**	• **Model, observe, and visit classrooms to inspect what we expect**	• Develop district capacity, trainers, champions, etc.
	• Celebrate improvement and professional growth	• Support a learning environment that is characterized by thinking outside the box and creativity
	• Provide accountability for achieving results	

(8) Student will utilize a range of appropriate tools (technology, manipulatives, etc.) to support the learning process and personalize learning.		
Teachers will:	**Building Administrators will:**	**District Office Admin. will:**
• Assign work via technology and/or requiring technology	• Model how to utilize a range of appropriate tools	• Provide PD for the assessment and use of a variety of tools
• Provide feedback and facilitate communication via technology	• **Access teacher needs to plan effective and personalized PD**	• Provide up-to-date and engaging tools for students and staff
• Attend PD to learn new technologies and/or research	• Provide time for teachers to research alternative tools	• **Allocate funds to best support the personalization of learning**
• Be lifelong learners in research technologies	• Provide feedback to teachers and students and families	• Provide feedback for principals and teachers
• Use data to inform instruction and personalize	• Use data to support the personalization of the learning process	
• **Access student learning styles and match with appropriate tools**		

AND BACKGROUND

The Every Student Succeeds Act (ESSA) is now the law of the land, replacing No Child Left Behind.

Appendix B
Sample Annual Report
M.S.D. of Warren Township
Second Annual District Report 2016-2017
The District Framework: Aligning Core Work
to District Goals

With ever changing requirements, this fourth annual report aims to summarize the progress made toward achieving the goals laid out in the District's Framework, as well as fulfilling of our final responsibilities as outlined in the federal Race To The Top Grant.

DISTRICT FRAMEWORK

Mission Statement:

Innovate at all times. Educate all. Inspire everyone to live a full and fulfilling life.

Warren's Personalized Learning Guiding Belief:

We are all learners who deserve personalized learning experiences to become leaders who have the skills to be successful in life and create solutions for a better tomorrow.

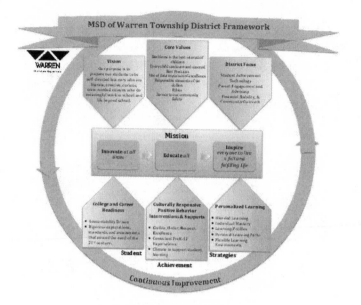

More specifically, the Warren Township goals for 2015 to 2018 are to:

(1) Build a personalized learning system through Blended Learning at all age levels.

(2) Prepare **all** students to be College and Career Ready by implementing the methods of Close Reading, Depth of Knowledge, Questioning and Text Complexity, and Mathematical Practices.

(3) Build Positive Behavior Interventions and Supports (PBIS) based upon the principles outlined in CORE (Civility, Order, Respect, Excellence) in Tier I, Tier II and Tier III.

The district framework has become the operating structure that guides all decision-making in the district. All staff can point to each element and see their place in our district thinking and our personalized learning strategy for themselves as well as for their students.

ACADEMIC FRAMEWORK

Year End Review

The purpose of Warren Township schools is to prepare our students to be self-directed learners who are creative, critical thinking, civic-minded, democratic citizens who do meaningful and productive work in both school and post-school life.

We are a part of an exciting shift occurring in schools across America, as teachers and administrators respond to the challenges and opportunities our children face in the 21st Century. Our school district is providing teachers and students with powerful new tools that enable personalized, student-centered learning by blending the best of face-to-face instruction with new technology. (Communications Planning for Innovation in Education. The Learning accelerator/ Education Elements 2015.

The 2016-17 school year was exciting as we continued to launched Personalized Learning through Blended Learning throughout the district and this year with a concentration on the high school. After years of coming to understand Personalized Learning, we continue to make iterations in our process now know how to explain it to our school community. We recognize 'personalized' as learning tailored to students' strengths, needs and interests, which includes encouraging voice and choice in what, how, when, and where they learn. Blended Learning leverages technology to create a learning environment where students have daily opportunities for individualized learning and teachers have the opportunities, resources, and time to differentiate targeted instruction in the classroom.

ESSA defines Digital/Blended learning as "any instructional practice that effectively uses technology to strengthen a student's learning experience and encompasses a wide spectrum of tools and practices." Included are the following:

- Interactive resources, digital content, software or simulations
- Access to online databases and primary documents
- Use of data and information to personalize learning and provide targeted supplementary instruction
- Online and computer-based assessments
- Learning environments that promote collaboration and communication

Blended learning is a formal education program in which a student learns, at least in part, through online delivery of content and instruction with some element of student control over time, place, and/or pace. With the help of our consultant Education Elements in Warren Township, we consider the following components to be a core part of Blended Learning: 1) Targeted instruction (full-class, small group or individual), 2) Integrated digital content, 3) Student reflection, and 4) Data driven decisions. Students are now more active and engaged participants of their own learning. Through Blended Learning, students have a voice and choice in group projects, online remediation, practice and/or enrichment through online or paper-and-pencil assignments.

In addition, as we move into blended learning through personalized learning the look and feel of the classroom and how instruction is delivered is changing. The roles of teachers and students are shifting as we make this adjustment. We continue to support both students and teachers with change PBIS, and teaching expectations of new spaces, new activities and new programs is more important than ever. The intentional teaching, practicing, reinforcing and then re-teaching of behavioral and academic expectations is supporting the changes in the classroom.

Our personalized learning mid-year report from April 13, 2016 provided useful reflections for the district leadership team as our consultant took a snapshot of our personalized learning progress. Some of the successes noted in the mid-year report are as follows:

1. School Personalized Learning (PL) teams are truly leading the work.
2. The PL rollout has embodied the district belief statement "we all deserve PL."
3. The district leadership team has done an incredible job listening and responding to the needs of schools.
4. Communication and sharing is happening within and cross cohorts.

Education Elements suggested the following as next steps in moving forward:

1. Ensure schools move beyond the "checklist approach" for deeper understanding and implementation of the core four
2. Personalized PD
3. Refresh digital content tools.

Successes

Our first success of 2015-2016 was another 90% graduation rate.

This spring, the IREAD-3 test scores were the highest in our previously lowest performing schools where assistant superintendents had placed intentional and targeted interventions.

Sunny Heights Elementary scored 88%, an increase of 16% and Brookview remained steady at 85%.

The CORE-PBIS framework continues to support student-centered environments by teaching students what our expectations are in **all** learning environments. This includes common areas such as cafeterias, hallways, restrooms, but also for classroom procedures such as independent work, small group, project work, etc. By teaching students what we expect of them and allowing them to practice, we are providing them a foundation, enabling them to fully participate in academic instruction.

Tier 1 is actively implemented in all schools and our S.E.T evaluations, performed by outside evaluators, showed 15 schools that are successfully implementing, with fidelity, PBIS performance measures. An important key to success in the area of PBIS was understanding the need to pace the roll out of Tier 2 to correspond to individual school needs. We did a district wide roll out of Tier 1, which we believe to be the best decision. However, when implementing Tier 2 we realized some buildings were ready before others. After providing the initial training for everyone, we could then support the schools with rolling out as they were ready, giving both the school and students a better likelihood of success.

The Blended Learning implementation took considerable planning and preparation prior to the January launch of Cohort I. Our consultation with Education Elements ensured a smooth transition as we transformed learning for students in five Cohort 1 Blended Learning schools. District and building leaders are to be commended for helping their respective communities make the necessary adjustments.

The use of digital content is helping to determine "what works" for personalized learning through Blended Learning, and the result is that we no longer have to wait for 3-week assessment data to determine next steps in instruction. Teachers now have access to digital content in which they can make instructional decisions for students in a matter of minutes, hours, or days depending on the project, assignment, or performance task.

While the achievements discussed above are encouraging, perhaps a stronger indication of the successful climate in Warren Township is demonstrated by the level of excellence our students and individual schools demonstrate in a multitude of areas. The list below gives the major highlights:

- Brookview was named a Promising Practice school by the Indiana Department of Education.
- Grassy Creek Robotics Team placed 2nd at the state finals. They attended the World competition placing 16th in the World!
- The Nanoline Team from the Walker Career Center placed 1st in the State Pre-Engineering competition and won a trip to Disney Land.
- The Department of Education announced the Walker Career Center as part of the first cohort of STEM certified schools in the state.
- Gold Brigade Marching Band earned 1st place at Greenfield High School.
- Student Council HUAH collected 16,781 items for Sonny Day food pantry.
- Warren Wrestling team won State for the first time since 1980.
- Warren Township School district received an Inspire and Engage Award at the Personalized Learning Summit in May in San Francisco
- Warren Township was also granted a 2016 Best Communities for Music Award.
- Finally, our girl's track team was recently crowned state champions!

Challenges

The body of work our teachers and staff engaged in started with the long-term effort to personalize learning within the new Indiana Academic Standards. The initiatives have included: student voice and choice, personalized PD for teachers, integration of technology and new digital content, redesigned instructional calendars, assessments, and moving to a middle school English Language Arts 100-minute block.

Next year, we will add additional time to our math block, which will move to 80 minutes and decrease the time of ELA by ten minutes. Four strategies we will use to increase knowledge and understanding as we teach the new Indiana College and Career Readiness Standards are: Close Reading, Depth of Knowledge, deeper levels of thinking through Questioning, and Text Complexity. In sum, the district staff was given a huge challenge to reinvent how teachers deliver instruction in this new educational environment.

This year most of the formative assessments and performance tasks were done paper-pencil style with a few being completed online using the Socrative platform. We have purchased a data warehouse that is compatible with Tyler called DecisionEd, which will house all of the district, teacher, and student data in real time.

As mentioned before, our PBIS S.E.T evaluations show the majority of our schools being successful, but two schools were found to be in need of a restart and those schools are now working more diligently with our district team. We are also evaluating a decrease in IREAD-3 scores of our traditionally high performing schools to determine the root causes of suspected changes.

Achievement Across Framework Dimensions

The District Framework provides the focus and structure for our work, and also functions as a roadmap. Intentional plans along with intentional goals are necessary. To that end, we have continued to concentrate in the four key areas listed below. Under each category we have supplied data to support the level of success for each initiative thus far.

1. Personalized Learning – Transforming teaching and learning for students through the use of the Blended Learning data based system;
2. College and Career Ready – Technical training, dual credit, and Advanced Placement
3. Technology Integration – Digital content alignment and utilization
4. PBIS Culturally Relevant Teaching – CORE, Tier I PBIS implementation district-wide, with training for Tier II implementation

Personalized Learning

According to Knowledge Works, As today's high schoolers graduate from high school and continue on to community college, and four year college, and certificate program, or a new career, they will be preparing for a workplace that continues to change dramatically due to rapid advances in technology and innovation cycles. However, their schools remain largely the same, with teachers being the sole drivers of curriculum delivery and differentiated supports and interventions. We have been working for the past three years to ensure our teachers are provided the professional development needed to transform their classrooms to meet the need of the next generation/21st Century students.

Our top priorities are improving both academic achievement and social competence. This will enable all our students to compete in an uncertain and ambiguous world. Using personalized Blended Learning is how we are tackling our goal of academic achievement.

Evidence of success in the area of personalized learning is demonstrated through teacher and student feedback as well as some promising NWEA trends. In the spring of 2016, 2,831 students and 336 teachers took a survey that asked about core elements of personalized learning, including small group instruction and student reflection. Responses came from all 17 schools. The goal of this survey was to articulate a general trend of teacher and student experiences of, and attitudes toward, personalized learning. We saw four positive trends in the survey responses:

CI Teachers Feel They Can Differentiate More
97% of CI teachers agree that they are able to provide more differentiated instruction with PL*

CI Teachers Think Students Are More Engaged
~80% of CI teachers agree that their students are more engaged, yet only about half of all students feel that school is personalized to what they like and need*

Small Group Instruction Increasing In IA/MS
CI intermediate/middle school teachers are ~30% more likely to use small group instruction every day or a few times a week than their CII peers

Teachers Are Confident + Enjoy Teaching PL
88% of teachers are confident in a BL approach for their school and ~60% of teachers agree that they enjoy teaching more or feel more effective teaching since implementing PL

As Warren completed the first winter and spring NWEA Measures of Academic Progress (MAP), across grades K-8 we saw some positive trends in terms of Cohort I (who launched in January 2016) and Cohort II (who will launch in August 2016).

Specifically:

- In math, slightly more students at Cohort I schools met or exceeded expected growth than at Cohort II schools
- In reading, roughly the same portion of students met or exceeded expected growth at Cohort I and Cohort II schools
- All Intermediate Academies are Cohort I schools, so they have no direct comparison, but performance in grades 5 and 6 looks robust in math and on trend in reading, when compared to the general trend in performance from lower to higher grades.

College and Career Ready- The Walker Career Center was part of the first cohort of STEM certified schools recognized by the Indiana Department of Education. In 2016, we had 946 dual credits earned at the high school, and 3099 credits earned at the Walker Career Center. The table below demonstrates the steady increase in students taking advantage of this beneficial program.

Duel Credit History			
	2015-2016	2014-2015	2013-2014
Fall	319	251	269
Spring	627	592	368
Total	946	843	668
Percent Increase	12%	26%	N/A

Other impressive statistics include:

• 424 certifications at the Walker Career Center, which represents an increase of 100 students.

• For the second year in a row the graduation rate at 90%.

• 118 students at the high school and career center were selected to explore and participate in Extended Learning Opportunities (ELOs) with business partners in the community.

• 190 students earn their HSE (GED) through WWC's Adult Education evening program.

• For students not interested in attending college after graduation, we also held a job fair at the high school for approximately 200 students. It is our hope to keep students involved as active participants in their community.

One area where we can increase our efforts is in the number of students taking Advanced Placement courses. This number was down 56 students from the previous year, and we believe the drop is due to the increase in the number of students taking advantage of the dual credit options at the high school and career center. We will continue to help students make choices that will enable them to succeed in their chosen future path.

Technology Integration

We are experiencing an era of unbelievable technological advancement. At the rate new programs and opportunities are presenting themselves, the task of choosing highly effective digital tools can be daunting. Warren Township has thoughtfully chosen various digital initiatives to implement throughout the district. The table below gives a breakdown of these digital tools and shows the percentage of students actively engaged in the targeted grade levels.

Flexible Curriculum Platform Utilization					
Program Name	Subject Area	Grade Level	Students Active	Total Students	Percent Active
Lexia	Reading	Elementary	4229	4964	85%
Ten Marks	Math	Elementary/ Intermediate	3134	5645	56%
Achieve3000	Reading	Intermediate/ Middle	2995	3623	83
ST Math	Math	Elementary/ Intermediate/ Middle	5369	8266	65%
Compass		Elementary/ Intermediate/ Middle	5425	7431	73%

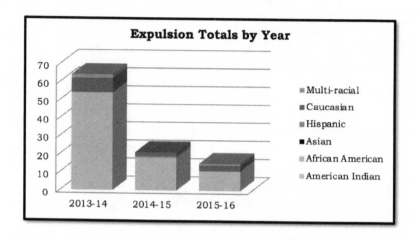

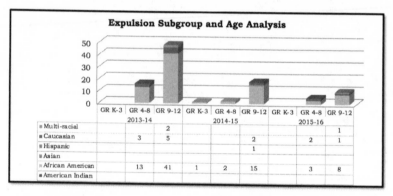

	GR K-3	GR 4-8	GR 9-12	GR K-3	GR 4-8	GR 9-12	GR K-3	GR 4-8	GR 9-12
		2013-14			2014-15			2015-16	
Multi-racial			2						1
Caucasian	3	5				2		2	1
Hispanic						1			
Asian									
African American	13	41	1	2	15			3	8
American Indian									

PBIS Culturally Relevant Teaching

CORE goals, strategies and projects for PBIS implementation were developed with input from district administrators, principals, teachers, and parents and draw heavily from Race To the Top milestones and deliverables. Tier I implementation has commenced and there is clear evidence in the vast reduction of both referrals and expulsions that PBIS is having the desired impact. Since 2013, the rate of expulsions has dropped by 77% from 64 expulsions to 15. The charts below detail these results.

District Performance Measures

Curricular Evaluating and Selection

Ensuring quality performance, and effectiveness are the cornerstones of excellence. The district revised practices that integrate the development of instructional calendars in the content areas of science and social studies. ELA calendars K-12 were also added to ensure learning progression sequences are developmentally and grade level appropriate.

After a year of piloting math curriculum, the district selected Eureka math at the K-6 levels and Agile Minds for grades 7-12. With this new, more rigorous, curriculum we are providing numerous professional development opportunities for teachers during the school day and on weekends. The district continues to seek and research effective educational practices that integrate high quality instruction, rigorous instructional calendars and assessments, personalized learning through Blended Learning and 21st Century skills. We continue to understand that a persisting culture of collaboration must be present in every aspect of the educational program and that CORE, a culture of care, continues to be demonstrated daily throughout the district.

Teacher Evaluating Practices

We have standards to hold students to, we mapped out pathways for each quarter, students have to be introduced to materials, be they can still work on earlier content. We have individualized playlists. In each playlist, there are assessments integrated for each playlist.

Conditions:

In a personalized learning classroom, teachers bring the curriculum and aligned tools to life for their students. According to interviews with teachers, the curriculum must be grounded in a personalized learning vision aligned at the school and district levels, and it must be flexible enough to meet the changing needs of students. With a personalized approach, teachers are surrounded by data and must be able to identify what data to closely analyze and organize around. As a result teachers are better able to develop, review, and adjust curricular materials in response to the real-time, needs of their students.

In a personalized system, teachers work with students to shape the curriculum, by identifying the path to mastery in the appropriate order with a focus on building both knowledge and skills. While there is no negotiation around which standards students need to meet, they are allowed flexibility, around time and demonstration of mastery, in how they engage with the curriculum. Students' voices are involved in creating individual learning pathways 2015, Knowledge Works Jenkins, William, Moyer, George and Foster.

The M.S.D of Warren Township's Teacher Evaluation Assessment Model (TEAM) document is a means by which high-quality instruction and performance is evaluated. In 2011, Warren Township was selected by the Indiana Department of Education to develop a "pilot" evaluation tool along with six other districts in the state. M.S.D Warren Township worked collaborative with the teachers union (WEA) to create our customized evaluation tool to meet the new requirements of SEA.

This year 98.5% of our Warren Township teachers were rated Effective or Highly Effective.

In an effort to prepare administrators for the evaluation document, all K-12 principals read *Drive* by Daniel Pink, and *Visible Learning for Teachers* by John Hattie. With new administrators at five buildings, we will provide extra support through individual and group training presented by retired principals.

School Evaluating Practices

District performance measures that gauge progress towards attaining our goals within each core work area were reviewed. The district report card identifies performance measures that indicate both a desired outcome and the degree to which individual schools and the district are making progress towards meeting those goals. Our district report card measures progress towards creating students prepared for college and the workforce. The school reports this year were reviewed and recognized by the Board of Education and monetary incentives awarded to schools meeting Report Card performance measures. The report card is updated and reviewed annually, through this and other documents as required by the state of Indiana.

In addition, Focus (D) rated schools will continue to be monitored through state and district accountability measures. We will continue the use of SMART Goals and turnaround principles as prescribed by State guidelines for Focus schools. The eight principles are: 1) School Leadership 2) School Climate and Culture 3) Effective Instruction 4) Curriculum, Assessment, and Intervention System 5) Effective Staffing Practices 6) Enabling the Effective Use of Data 7) Effective Use of Time and 8) Effective Family and Community Engagement. The report card uses the following assessments to measure the degree to which individual schools and the district are accomplishing the five items:

Report Card Focus Area	Assessment
Personalized learning	The level at which "Student Will" behaviors are enacted to increase student voice and choice
Graduation rate	Graduation rate (target improvement 88%-90%)
Reducing the Achievement Gap	Blended learning data, monthly district assessments and performance tasks K-12. Targeted- Integrated digital content
Student Literacy	Performance on the Indiana IREAD-3 assessment. IREAD-3 spring and summer data
College and Career Readiness	College and career dual credit and certifications rate above 25%

Benchmarks For Instruction

College and Career Readiness benchmarks for instruction and student achievement (calendars and assessments) have been redesigned by the district and can be provided to stakeholders in snapshot form upon request. The purpose of the calendar and benchmark assessments is to provide a clear view of college and career readiness starting in PreK-10. In addition, these assessments will enable teachers, parents and students to monitor students' progress from a very early age and adjust programming as needed to ensure continuous improvement on a quarterly and annual basis. Grades 11-12 will use benchmark data to measure success from SAT/ACT, Advanced Placement Exams and future graduation rates.

Plans for Improvement

The district's continuous improvement platform (outlined below) provides the foundation for improvement. The pursuit of excellence is part of Warren's DNA. The goal of the Continuous Improvement Process is to drive improved instruction and student outcomes. In their book, *School Leadership that works*, Marzano, Waters & McNulty (2005) define continuous improvement as, "the continual and incremental-complex improvement of the critical aspects of the organization" (p.16). Continuous Improvement is a simple concept: *keep working to make things better and never give up.*

The Continuous Improvement Process provides teachers and principals with a consistent framework for planning and provides clarity around their roles. Big changes will occur as we transform the process and we will be challenged to expand on this time tested strategy. Race To the Top provided the fuel and the focus to enter the next phase of improvement for Warren students.

"When continuous improvement becomes embedded in a system's culture, it functions as 'the guiding force that keeps the schools on target in an uncompromising quest for quality at every corner of the district." (Zmuda, Kuklis & Klein, 2004, p.6)

Continuous Improvement Process

PLAN
Constant Data Review
Student test scores are used to identify instructional groups and to identify strong and weak curriculum areas and practices. Flexible grouping provides the necessary level of instructional support for mastery of standards. 1) Enhancing assessments 2) Increasing Data Access 3) Collecting new types of data 4) investing in staff learning

Instructional Timeline/Calendars
A timeline that encompasses all college-and career ready standards serve as a guide for instruction based on the need of the student group and the weight of the standard/objective/project. 1) Redesigning Curriculum, 2) Shifting to Common Core

ACT
Adjust Instruction/ Tutorials
Teacher teams (PLC's)/(Learning Log) and key stakeholders collaborate to reflect on assessment data for the purpose of adjusting instruction to personalize student learning. 1) Increase learning options for students 2) Deliver curriculum through digital age tools

Personalized Interventions and Enrichment STEAM activity
Provide intervention/time to re-teach non-mastered targeted College and Career Ready standards and STEAM opportunities for both mastery and non-mastery whenever possible.
*Adaptive software identified to provide a personalized intervention path.

DO
Instructional Focus Student and Teacher Facilitated
Using the timeline, instruction is delivered using multiple pathways, to address the unique learning interest, needs and pace of each student. Technology enhances personalize learning. 1) Increasing Personalization of Learning 2) Expanding Learning Time & Ensuring Relevance of Learning 3) Initiating Online Learning Options

CHECK
Assessment
District provides high quality assessments that are administered to identify intentional next step when mastery and non-mastery is attained. 1) Enhance assessment tools 2) Improving feedback for teachers, students, and parents

Intentional Maintenance
Based on individual student need, intentional and consistent maintenance of college and career ready standards through personalized digital content. 1) Enlisting parents as partners 2) Upgrading technology for digital age learning

Monitor
Continuously monitor and evaluate the process/progress of student achievement. 1) Examining responses to student behavior 2) Building strong connections with all students 3) Ensuring grant activities are successful 4) Analyzing data trends

Coherence (Personalization)

— Superintendent — Technology infrastructure

— "How do we make up the Covid learning loss?"

— Innovate Educate Inspire